God's Glory...
Man's is Dust

An Overview of Reformed Theology

Win Groseclose

God's Glory...Not Man's
© 2014, Win Groseclose

ISBN: 978-1-312-40901-9

Unless otherwise noted, all scripture quotations are the author's translation from the Greek or Hebrew.

Cover Photo: The Reformation Wall,
Geneva, Switzerland
(Depicting William Farel, John Calvin, Theodore Beza, & John Knox)
© Elenarts - fotolia.com

Published by Lulu.com

Dedicated to Rick Burnor, Charles Wilson, and Derek Thomas.

Rick, you were my first mentor and guide not only in terms of my introduction to Reformed theology, but also in terms of my coming to faith. Thank you for opening your home to this student that did not know his right hand from his left.

Charles, your preaching inspired and moved me in ways that I had not been moved before. You proclaimed God's sovereignty in your preaching and that preaching had power. Thank you.

Derek, aside from being a mentor and putting up with many questions from a new seminary student, you opened a door for me and introduced me to many ministers and theologians of the past that have proven to me faithful friends... I am especially grateful for your introducing me to Dr. Lloyd-Jones. It is also your introductory lecture outlines that I "borrowed" in 2005 when I was first given the invitation to teach the TULIP to seminary students in Ukraine. My hope is that you are honored by what those lectures have grown into.

הוֹי רָב אֶת־יֹצְרוֹ
חֶרֶשׂ אֶת־חַרְשֵׂי אֲדָמָה

Table of Contents

Chapter 1: So What? 5

Chapter 2: The Bad News First 9

Chapter 3: Setting a High Bar 15

Chapter 4: Triangles 21

Chapter 5: Flying Solo 25

Chapter 6: Caffeine for the Spirit 29

Chapter 7: The Roots of the Tulip 37

Chapter 8: The Bus and the Limo 49

Chapter 9: Total Depravity 59

Chapter 10: Unconditional Election 67

Chapter 11: Limited Atonement 77

Chapter 12: Irresistible Grace 91

Chapter 13: The Perseverance of the Saints 95

Chapter 14: Apples and Peaches and Worldview Changes 105

Chapter 15: God Initiates; Man Responds (Ordo Salutis) 111

Chapter 16: Trial by Fire — The Work of Sanctification 117

Chapter 17: One People: Two Covenants 123

Chapter 18: Credo, Ergo Confiteor 131

Chapter 19: Just the Beginning 137

Introduction

So, why another book on Reformed Theology? It seemed that after teaching this material for the past seven or eight years in a mission seminary in Ukraine, it was an appropriate time for me to re-work some of the material that I teach to seminarians and present it in a way that would be helpful to those people who are sitting in the pews: particularly those of you who happen to be sitting in the pews under my preaching. The ideas put together in this volume shape how I look at scripture and thus how it is taught and preached — more importantly, these ideas shape how I believe life is to be lived out before the face of God — and not just my life, but the lives of you who sit in the pews as well.

I could say that I also have a rather unique view on some of these ideas. Having grown up in the United Methodist church, Reformed theology hasn't always been part of my thought process. In fact, my first exposure to Reformed teachings came when I was befriended by a Christian philosophy professor at the state university I was attending and we began discussing what the Bible taught on the idea of predestination. The next main influence was a pastor-friend of mine in the Methodist church who preached the sovereignty of God with a power and conviction that I had not seen in the Methodist ministers that I had listened to up until that point. Thus, there was Rick and Charles respectively who planted seeds, but the seeds did not prove to take root until I personally began to preach.

I had begun exploring my call into ministry and, at the time, had concluded that God's call was to be in business and not in ministry. You need to understand that I am a third-generation preacher, so I knew full well what life as a minister would entail. Needless to say, I had a wise mentor who insisted that I at least become licensed to preach so that I could continue to try my gifts.

He was insistent and I conceded to grant his wish. The Methodist church has a program where you can become licensed to preach, largely for pastors who are sick or on vacation, and thus I embarked on a new stage of my life, one that would last for five years, and one where my theology would gradually change so that when I arrived at the point when I stopped fighting God's call and began making plans for semunary, all I knew is that I was no longer a fit within Wesleyan circles. I did not realize it at the time, but I had become Reformed in my process of preparing and preaching sermons over that five years.

At the time, a friend of mine was also looking at seminaries and when he shared with me one of the schools he was considered, I went online and fell in love. I began discovering people who thought the same way I thought about God's word, but who had done so in a fuller and deeper way than I had ever dreamed. In God's providence, I had found my home in the Reformed faith.

As I said, in some ways this gives me a unique perspective on some of these matters — I have been on both sides of the debate. Yet, as I have found, I am not alone in having walked this path; many, many people have made the same transition as I did as they committed themselves to the study of scripture because, as I deeply believe, this is what the Bible teaches if the Bible is allowed to speak for itself. This does not mean that I do not respect those from my Methodist roots that have helped to shape me (and who still shape me in some ways), but I am convinced that many of the answers to essential questions cannot be answered satisfactorily by those who hold consistently to their Wesleyanism. This does not make their answers heretical, but I do believe that their answers are often unhelpful if one is seeking to be, as John Wesley would word it, "a Bible Christian." I desire to be a Bible-Christian — not almost, but fully — and as a result of that desire, God took me on a journey from one school of theological thought to another, and for that I am grateful.

Yet, I have made another journey as well, though this second journey is not nearly as broad. For the first ten years of my time in the Reformed church, I identified as a Presbyterian — though I confess, there were times when, to raise the hackles of my Methodist friends, I would identify as a Calvinist-Methodist in the tradition of George Whitefield! We will talk about Whitefield later on in this book, but let it be said that he retained his Calvinism while embracing both the outdoor style of preaching later associated with Wesley as well as the methodical approach to sanctification that Wesley also insisted upon.

Three years ago, though, I accepted a call to serve an old German Reformed congregation that was once part of the German Evangelical Protestant movement in the 1800s. This movement thrived in the Ohio River Valley region in the U.S. for about 100 years, but fell apart as churches joined with other denominations; our church being a last remnant. This movement accomplished something that few Christian movements have been able to accomplish. Here there was a group of German Reformed Christians and German Lutheran Christians gathering together for worship. Neither compromised their theological distinctions, but agreed that their differences were not such that would divide them in worship. Notice, they did not seek a middle-position of compromise, instead they passionately disagreed but maintained fellowship in the midst of disagreement. This tension was originally tried in Germany, it was the basic reason that the Heidelberg Catechism was written, but it did not find fertile soil until it was planted in America.

Thus, I found myself in a congregation that was German Reformed in its theology (having embraced Heidelberg as their primary doctrinal statement) but that had some Lutheran influences in areas of worship. Thus, my second journey came as I began to appreciate some of the nuances between Continental Reformed thought and the Presbyterian Reformed thought that I had embraced in seminary and also how those distinctions helped to shape the culture of this region of Western Pennsylvania.

And that brought about another reason for this book — a desire that those within my own flock (and any others as well) understand the basic system of theology that has shaped their heritage as a congregation. It is my conviction that one needs to know from where they have come to be able to remain steady on the path that God is calling them to walk. The purpose of this book is not to explain our congregational vision, but it is to lay out those cobblestones upon which we will walk as we pursue that vision in life — all to the glory of Christ and with gratitude for those people that Christ has brought into my life that have prodded me and walked alongside of me during these journeys.

—Win Groseclose, August 2014

CHAPTER 1

"SO WHAT?"

For many people, the "so what" question is a conversation stopper. Statistically, I have been told, that most people stay connected to a congregation because of the friendships they make within that particular church, not because of the theology that is taught. There are exceptions to every rule, granted, and I guess that I am one of those exceptions.

I suppose the proper response to that statement is — "you better!" For if the pastor has no idea as to why he serves in one denomination as opposed to another, then perhaps it is time to worry. Yet, I believe that a congregation as a whole should also care — and in terms of the big things, my experience is that they do, they just may not have the theological vocabulary to express the differences — and perhaps that is one good reason to study theology.

But I think that there is a bigger reason. Theology comes from two Greek words being put together: θεός (theos — meaning "God") and λόγος (logos — meaning "word" or "stuff"). Thus, putting the ideas together, Theology is the study of God ... or perhaps we could more literally say, "stuff about God." C.S. Lewis used to define theology as "God-Talk," which conveys the same basic idea. The bottom line is that those things we know about God are properly called (in a broad sense), "Theology."

And lo and behold, this God, who created everything there is, from the smallest mitochondria to the largest galaxy in space — to you and me — has decided not only to create, but to make himself known. And he has done so in a book — the Bible. Thus, while the secret things indeed do belong to God, that which he has revealed belongs to us and to our children through every generation.[1] This is the big reason — what better thing is there that we could study but the God who created us and who offers us redemption through his Son? The study of mathematics or history certainly does have its merits in this life, but the study of God has merits in the next life as well. God is the most wonderful of all persons thus a study of God is and cannot help but be the most wonderful of all studies that we could commit ourselves to.

But, let us not stop there. Not only does theology show us the character of the God we serve as Christians, it shows us how to live in a way that honors him. One of the traps that people fall into is doing theology simply for theology's sake — spending time in lofty speculation that never finds application in life. The reality is that every decision that we make in life is informed by the theology we believe — we will explore that idea further a little later on, but let it be said that one of the most practical reasons for the Christian to study theology is to help him or her know how to live life to its fullness.

There is one other reason to study theology that needs to be mentioned up front, and that is to establish a wall of protection for your faith and for the faith of your family. The bottom line is that there will always be people who will design to distort the theology of the church. A brief survey of church history ought to illustrate that principle with sobering clarity. Churches and denominations have drifted into liberalism and syncretism as well as accommodating the

---

[1] Deuteronomy 29:29.

things of the world — chasing after the spirit of the age instead of correcting it.

This shift toward liberalism does not happen overnight, but it instead tends to be a slow decline over a generation or more where people forget the tenets of their faith and who the God of their "God Talk" really happens to be. False teachers do not appear in church congregations wearing a long-red-pointed tail and carrying a pitchfork, they instead begin by infusing subtle errors into their teaching that lead people astray. Often those errors sound "almost-right" but have profound implications if taken to their logical end.

And thus, for your own spiritual health, for your family's spiritual health, and for your church's spiritual health the study of theology is a worthy pursuit for all who fill the pews on Sunday morning. Be like the faithful Bereans who, after hearing the Apostle Paul speak, went to the scriptures and examined everything he taught to confirm that it was true (Acts 17:10-11). The bottom line is that unless the theology of a congregation is guarded both from the pulpit and from the pew, it will likely drift into error to the detriment of all.

So, as we move forward and discuss Reformed theology, let us begin by setting forth a framework within which a healthy conversation can take place — ground rules, or marks that distinguish good theology from bad theology.

CHAPTER 2

THE BAD NEWS FIRST

"So, I have some good news and some bad news; which do you want to hear first?" Isn't that always the dilemma that we face in life? So, why not get the bad news over with up front? Usually things are easier if you do it that way...

Wait a minute, though, is preference the only reason to talk about the marks of bad theology before the marks of good theology? No, not at all. Sometimes, in order to better understand what something is, it is valuable to understand what something is not. And thus, in setting forth the "is nots" of theology, it will help us better understand what good theology is. With that in mind, we set forth four marks of bad theology.

DEAD ORTHODOXY

Really, this phrase is a bit of an oxymoron. "Orthodoxy" means "correct doctrine," and if one's doctrine is correct, their spiritual life ought to be vibrant and anything but "dead." But something happens sometimes in a person's life, when they become so focused on the letter of the law and they forget the principle behind the law. This often takes place when the zeal to be "right" becomes so strong that one condemns any dissenting opinions and embraces one form of legalism or another. How often, Christians have divided over whether one ought to use risen or un-risen bread for the Lord's table, whether psalmnody alone is proper in worship or whether hymns (and praise songs) are permissible, or over which translation of the Bible that someone might prefer. The Apostle John reminds us that true children of God show their faith as they love the brotherhood.[2] This does not mean that we abandon truth or compromise it, but it does mean that when we approach another professing Christian who differs with us on their understanding that we do so with graciousness and love.

Historically, the Pharisees were a good example of this kind of dead orthodoxy. At their inception, the group had all of the best intentions. They saw the corruption that was entrenched in the Hasmonean Dynasty, and sought to bring reform by teaching the people to lead Godly lives. Yet, by Jesus' day, something had happened. They had created rule after rule to help them fulfill the letter of the Mosaic law. Yet, in seeking to fulfill the law, they missed the intent behind the law, which was to drive them to Christ.[3] Sadly, in missing Christ, these men became enemies of the people and of the Messiah, making disciples of hell rather than of God.[4]

There is another application of dead orthodoxy that is perhaps more common today and thus more dangerous: that of just "going through the motions." The church in Sardis was guilty of falling into this trap[5] — they had a good reputation for their works (in other words they were doing all of the right things) but Jesus judged them as being dead. Sometimes we believe that God will be pleased with us because we "do" all of the right things, yet as God

---

[2] 1 John 3:16-18.

[3] Galatians 3:24-25.

[4] Matthew 23:15.

[5] Revelation 3:1-4.

says so often in the prophets[6], your sacrifices are an abomination to me unless they begin with a heart of love and service. Not only is faith without works dead,[7] but works without faith is just as lifeless.

Wildfire Passion

In many ways, Wildfire Passion is the extreme opposite of Dead Orthodoxy. Here we find a passion for God that is without any focus or discipline, but simply rages about in every direction bringing destruction wherever it goes. If Dead Orthodoxy is a stumbling block when a pursuit of right doctrine is taken to an extreme, Wildfire Passion is a stumbling block when a pursuit of experience is taken to the extreme. If Dead Orthodoxy is the error into which Reformed Christians are sometimes prone to slide; wildfire passion tends to be the error of Pentecostalism when taken to the extreme.

Biblically, the church in Corinth was a good example of this error. They clearly were gifted by God in many ways, but the people ran amok with these gifts. As one reads the letters of Paul to this church, there was clearly no effective leadership, discipline, or direction within this congregation. Every man did as he desired and Paul was baffled by their conduct.[8]

For much of the watching world, what they know about Christ they will learn by watching the church act towards its members. If people see us as dead legalists, what does that say about the character of God? If people see us as chaotic and without direction, people will be inclined to think that God is the same way. Yet God is not a God of confusion.[9]

---

[6] Isaiah 1:11-20; Amos 5:21-24; Micah 6:6-8.

[7] James 2:17.

[8] 1 Corinthians 4:14-21.

[9] 1 Corinthians 14:33.

Vain Theology

Solomon begins his Apologetic work we know as Ecclesiastes with the words, "Vanity of vanities — all is vanity!" Indeed, to paraphrase him as he continues, the pursuit of vanity is like chasing after the wind. No matter how greatly you apply yourself, you will never wrangle it down because it doesn't have anything you can grab ahold of. Such is the vanity that accompanies one's efforts when their theology is driven by the whims of the culture or novelty.

How greatly people are drawn to the pull of popularity. People want book deals, television programming, and radio airtime. Pastors want the reputation of preaching before audiences of thousands rather than that of carefully shepherding a flock for a lifetime. And of course, this draw is nothing new as Paul warns Timothy that there are those coming that will be lovers of self and money and who will strive after knowledge but never arrive at truth.[10] How Paul sounds like Solomon when he writes.

In contrast to this way of the world, Job's companion, Elihu, points out that genuine understanding comes from the breath of the Almighty.[11] Thus, if we wish to have understanding in our Theology, we must appeal to the Scriptures, for they are θεόπνευστoß (theopneustos) — "God-Breathed."[12]

Sadly, another place that Vain Theology shows itself in modern culture is in scholarship. Grants and degrees are often awarded to those who propose theological ideas on the basis of their novelty rather than promoting sober scholarship.

---

[10] 2 Timothy 3:1-7.

[11] Job 32:8.

[12] 2 Timothy 3:16.

The Cult of Personality

The final mark of bad theology is that theology that is centered around a man rather than being centered around God. This theology is "anthro-centric" rather than being "theocentric" and leads into error. There is only one man — the God-Man, Jesus Christ — that our theology must be centered around, but how often this is not the case in our churches. Instead, people seek out pastors that suit their own passions or are celebrities of a sort.[13]

Isaiah reminds us that we are not to pay much regard to men, whose breath is in their noses[14], instead, we are to center our life and worship around the *God* who has made the man. Again, any theology or church that finds itself centered around a man falls into idolatry.

It would seem almost inevitable, given that we are a fallen people, that to some degree churches and theologians will fall into one of these traps if not more than one. The sign of the true Christian theologian and the true church is that they recognize those errors as errors, repent of them, and seek to turn away from the errors that they have committed. All too often, though, when error is confronted, excuses are made for said errors and no repentance is found. Such theology is not good theology at all. Of those who would promote such, one ought to accept the advice of the Apostle Paul and "avoid such people."[15]

---

[13] 2 Timothy 4:3-4.

[14] Isaiah 2:22.

[15] 2 Timothy 3:5.

Chapter 3
Setting a High Bar

As we transition from those things we are to avoid in our theology, we need to establish up front that no system of theology is perfect. We are fallen creatures and we are sinful. We make mistakes but hopefully learn from those mistakes. We must also learn from those Christians around us that have demonstrated Biblical wisdom and insight and we must learn from those godly theologians that have gone before us in history. Nevertheless, those marks listed here are marks that every system of Christian theology must strive toward so that it can be both understood and lived out in a way that does not lose sight of the one whom we worship.

It Must Be Biblically Accurate

The scriptures are the written revelation of the Almighty God given to us for training, edification, correction, and well…for all that we do.[16] That means the scriptures are not just a place to which

---

[16] 2 Timothy 3:16-17.

we go for prooftexts to prove our point, but the whole council of God is our judge and our rule by which we evaluate every idea and upon which we construct every doctrine. Without good exegesis[17], we do not have good theology. Our theology must begin where the scriptures begin and come to a close when the scriptures allow us to infer no more.

It Must Accurately Describe the World Around Us

Sir Francis Bacon is notable for stating: "God has, in fact, written two books, not just one. Of course, we are all familiar with the first book he wrote, namely Scripture. But he has written a second book called creation."[18] Indeed, we can learn of God in both places, though we must keep their relationship clear. What God offers in Scripture is authoritative and a rule by which all things are understood. What God offers in Creation is meant to be illustrative of what is revealed propositionally in Scripture. Or, perhaps one could word it this way: the Scriptures are the Words of God's book and nature are the illustrations within.

What that means for our theology, though, is that our theology cannot be at odds with the pictures of the world that God has given us. If we develop a theology, for example, from Philippians 4:13 that states since I can "do anything in Christ," it means I can ignore gravity and fly or that I can swim the Atlantic Ocean if I just have enough faith, then your theology is askew. Good theology must conform to the scriptures, but it also must accurately describe what

---

[17] Exegesis is the process of critically interpreting or explaining the text of Scripture — "what does it say?" It is the opposite of "Eisegesis" which is the process of reading your own ideas into scripture — "what do I want it to say?"

[18] Francis Bacon: "The Advancement of Learning."

we can learn by observation of the world around us.

It Must Be God-Centered

To borrow from C.S. Lewis, we must never forget the God behind the "God-Talk." The Bible begins with God as the subject and ends with God as the subject. God is the hero of scriptures as well as its author. It must never be forgotten that we exist to glorify God; God does not exist to glorify us.

It Must Be Christ-Centered

Not only should our theology be Theo-centric, it must be Christo-centric. All of the Bible, Jesus points out, is about him[19], thus all of our theology must also point to him. All of the Old Testament anticipates the coming of Christ and the New Testament is written as a result of Christ's coming. From beginning to end, things are about Jesus. Thus all of the promises of scripture find their meaning in Jesus Christ.[20] As Jesus is God, this certainly offers no conflict with our theological "God-centeredness" mentioned just before.

It Must Be Glorifying to God

In theological terms, we would say that good theology must be "doxological," meaning it must have "glorious words" of God. The Westminster Shorter Catechism, question 1, poses the question in this manner: "What is the chief end of man?" And the answer that

---

[19] Luke 24:27,44.
[20] 2 Corinthians 1:19-20.

follows: "The chief end of man is to glorify God and to enjoy him forever." Similarly, the Heidelberg Catechism asks, "What do we do that is good?" The answer: "Only that which arises out of true faith, conforms to God's law, and is done for his glory; and not that which is based on what we think is right or on established human tradition." God is worthy to be glorified as such and our theology needs to drive us toward that glory.

IT MUST BE ESCHATALOGICAL AND PROTOLOGICAL

When I was growing up, these were what was called "Twenty-five Cent Words." Even so, they are the best words to describe this next element that all good theology must strive toward. First, it must be Eschatalogical — in other words, it must look toward the end consummation of all things. We are reminded in scripture that there is a new heavens and earth upon which we are waiting as well as a resurrection to glory for the believers (as well as a resurrection to damnation for the unbelievers). Any theology that does not look clearly in that future direction is inadequate at best.

But looking forward is not the only thing a good theology must do — it must be Protological — it must look backwards as well. God has placed many signs within redemptive history that point toward the coming of Christ or toward the end times. In addition, scripture reminds us that those who remember God's mighty works are strengthened in their faith and those who forget will fall into sin.[21] It is only by understanding the earlier event that we will understand the later ones. Thus we must look backwards as well as forwards to inform our theology.

---

[21] Psalm 78:7; Judges 2:10.

It Must Be Ecclesiastical

There is a cultural trend today that seems to be trying to separate Christianity from the Church, yet Biblically, they are intertwined. Thus, a good theology must be Ecclesiastical, in other words, it must focus on the church for the church is the body of Christ in this world[22] and the Bride of Christ is the church.[23] Jesus' promise is to build a church[24] and thus any theology that neglects or minimizes the significance of the church is lacking and is ignoring the promise of Christ.

It Must Encourage Sanctification

Salvation is not just about providing a way for fallen humans to go to heaven — it is about remaking us into the image of Christ. Thus, we are called to "be holy as God is holy."[25] That work of making us holy is what we refer to as sanctification — it is a work that God the Holy Spirit primarily does, but it is something that we also participate in. We will discuss this further when we talk about a Reformed perspective on Sanctification, but let it be said that if your theology does not drive you to put sin to death, then something is very wrong. Paul describes the transformation we undergo as a form of metamorphosis[26], and indeed it is, for it is the putting to death of the old man and embracing the new man that God has made in Christ.[27] Sanctification is not a work that will be completed in this

---

[22] 1 Corinthians 12:27; Ephesians 4:12.
[23] Matthew 9:15; Revelation 19:7-8.
[24] Matthew 16:18.
[25] 1 Peter 1:14-16; Leviticus 11:44.
[26] Romans 12:2.
[27] 2 Corinthians 5:17.

earthly life, but it is indeed a work that should be progressively seen in the life of the believer as he hungers and thirsts for righteousness.[28]

IT MUST ENCOMPASS ALL OF LIFE

Not only must our theology accurately describe the world around us, it must also address every area of our lives. We have a tendency to compartmentalize our lives into specific areas: this applies to my career, this applies to my home-life, and this applies to my time at church, etc… Yet, good theology does not lend itself to compartmentalization because God is not interested in a segment of your life; he is interested in all of it…he demands all of it! Thus, good theology needs to overflow from one area of your life to another, not only informing every area, but linking them together in a way that breaks down the artificial boundaries that we place in our lives.

As mentioned before, no system of theology will ever perfectly excel in all of these areas, but all systems of theology should strive to excel in them. If, as you examine your theology, you realize that one of these areas is being ignored or is not present, this is an opportunity to examine why this area is not being striven toward and then to correct that path. We are frail and fallen, but God is patient and shows grace to those who repent of their error and pursue him.

---

[28] Matthew 5:6.

CHAPTER 4
TRIANGLES

What? Triangles? So, is this some sort of Trinitarian analogy that we are going to discuss next? No, not at all, it is a philosophical paradigm of looking at starting points that can be very helpful not only when examining ourselves but also when examining the views of others. Now, if any of my old High School Philosophy students are reading this, I expect that about now they are groaning a bit, because the triangle can be somewhat abstract, but be patient, in the end I suspect you will find it useful.

So imagine for a moment a perfect equilateral triangle — each side being the same length with each corner representing a 60 degree angle. For ease of description, imagine too that the top of the triangle is pointed up with the other two points on the bottom — somewhat like a single side of a pyramid. So far, so good?

Now, imagine that each of the three points of the triangle represents different approaches to human reasoning. Yet, the points themselves represent extremes. Normally human beings do not think at one of the extreme points, yet we all bias toward one of those given points. One might be tempted to argue that Adam and Eve were the perfect middle of the diagram and that the reason we are biased is because of their fall. I am not so sure that this is the case. Likely a better way to describe our location on the triangle is that God created people differently and to be differently biased as to the triangle so as to compliment one another when we work together in fellowship. That said, those who press the extremes of their bias certainly do exist and it is their condition that can likely be attached to the Fall.

And, it should be noted that God is not in this triangle — it could not hold him. God is the creator of the triangle and the triangle is a finite representation of the thought processes created by an infinite God to honor him.

So, what kinds of philosophical starting points are presented on this triangle? There are three distinct approaches to interpreting knowledge: the Normative approach, the Teleological approach, and the Existential approach...

The Normative Approach

This approach judges all ideas and experiences according to an established or fixed norm. If the new idea conforms to the norm — in the Christian's case, Scripture — then it is considered acceptable. If the experience or idea does not conform to the established norm, then the idea or experience is deemed in error and is rejected. The strength of this view ought to be obvious in that it recognizes the role of scripture to be the rule and measure of all things with which man engages. The weakness of this position is that it can lead to a form of legalism when pressed to the extreme.

The Teleological Approach

Telos is the Greek word for "end or purpose," and thus this approach tends to look at ideas and experiences in a more pragmatic light. "What is the purpose or end result of this line of action," or more simply, "Does this work?" are questions that those holding to this starting point will often ask. The strength of this starting point is that it often appeals to common sense and practical reason. The weakness of this starting point is that it can lead one to the presumption that the end justifies the means, in contradiction to Scriptural teachings.

The Existential Approach

This approach begins with one's personal interaction and response to an idea. "How do I feel about this?" and "Does this fit my experience?" are some of the first questions that one who holds the Existential approach will ask. The clear danger of this is that this view is prone toward subjectivism as is easily demonstrated in a survey of post-modern thought. At the same time, experience does have a valuable place in our reasoning process and the strength of this view is that it keeps this reality of personal experience with ideas in front of our minds.

The importance of understanding these three starting points for processing information should be obvious. None of us are absolutely in any one given corner, nor ought we be as that would lead us into error. We all have a bias. In knowing your own bias it hopefully will make you more intentional about thinking through ideas from all angles. In addition, understanding the starting point of one with whom you are speaking helps you understand how to communicate your ideas in a way that will be meaningful and persuasive to the listener. In the end, a balanced community needs to represent people of all three starting points and our theology needs to be able to be expressed in a meaningful way to those who hold to various points on the triangle.

CHAPTER 5
FLYING SOLO

No, being a theologian does not mean one must pass a pilot's exam (good thing!). But the early Reformers articulated five essential elements that marked their separation from the Roman Church — five areas where there could be no compromise and where the Roman church would have to meet them if the Roman church was to reform. The word "solo" is derived from the Latin word, "Solus," meaning "alone." Thus, these five points that separated (and still separate) the protestants from the Roman Catholics were known as the "Five Solae."

SOLA FIDE

Salvation is by Faith Alone. No good works, no good record with the church, no amount of money, or prestige, nor high or low birth can bring about salvation. The Roman church in Luther's day believed that it was the church that held the keys to the Kingdom of Heaven and thus God entrusted to the church and to her sacraments the power to commit people to or bar people from heaven eternally.

That is why people took the idea of excommunication so seriously, for they were taught that if the church removed you from her communion, you were eternally condemned to the fires of hell.

The Reformers understood that this mindset was nothing more than a tool of the Roman church to hold power over the minds and fears of the people of their day — remember, most people could not read the scriptures anyway as they were in Latin, so they could not challenge this idea on their own. But the Reformers were students of the scriptures and made the scriptures accessible to the people in their native tongues. And more importantly, they understood that the only works involved in salvation was the work of Jesus Christ, the God-man. And as Paul writes, it is not the human will or the works we might chase after, but it is on God and his mercy that salvation finds its rest.[29]

Sola Gratia

And that leads us to "Grace Alone." If salvation rests entirely on God and his good mercy and providence, and has nothing to do with us, then it is only by grace that we are saved. In fact, that is exactly what Paul writes as well: if works were a part of our salvation, then grace would no longer be grace.[30] Thus, even faith becomes a gift from God and not of our own doing.

Solo Christo

Even without a study of Latin, it is likely that one will recognize this third of the solae — "Christ Alone." Salvation comes

---

[29] Romans 9:16.
[30] Romans 11:6.

to us through the work of Christ alone. It does not come through the church or its sacraments nor is it worked by sacrifices or by priests. Salvation was accomplished by Jesus Christ alone — he did all of the work and we gain all of the benefits — in theological language, the atonement was a vicarious one.

SOLA SCRIPTURA

The Scriptures alone form the standard upon which our faith, our tradition, our theology, and our church stands and is judged. Again, the Roman church elevated the interpretations of councils and of Popes and place their interpretations as the only authoritative interpretation in the church. The reformers saw through this error and recognized that the fallenness of men means we make errors and mistakes, but the perfection of God means that the Scriptures are above all possibility of error and thus the proper and correct rule by which our thinking and practice is to be judged — they are the "Norma Absoluta"[31] of our faith.

There is a very important principle that comes out of this phrase that instructs us. When scripture is at odds with my experience or my ideas, it is my experience and ideas that must conform to scripture and not scripture to my ideas One very prevalent example in our culture is that over the creation versus evolution debate. Too many people try and demonstrate a harmony between scripture and science by reinterpreting their scriptures to match the scientific findings of the day. Instead, those scientific findings ought to be reinterpreted in light of the scriptural truth. I am capable of much error; God is not capable of any.

---

[31] "absolute norm" — Scripture is the final arbiter for faith and practice.

Sola Deo Gloria

All of this is for the Glory of God Alone. We have already discussed the importance of good theology being doxological; in the era of the Reformers especially, things were done for the glory and advancement of the church as an institution — the church became self-seeking and corrupt, being more concerned about its own glory instead of the glory of God. All that we do and all that God does is for his glory and not ours.

These five ideas became the battle cry of the Protestant Reformation and they definitely must remain core principles of our theology if we are going to remain Protestant and Biblical.

CHAPTER 6
CAFFEINE FOR THE SPIRIT

I confess that, like many Americans, my "drug of choice" is caffeine — in my case, by way of cups of hot tea. My personal confessions to the side, caffeine is a natural stimulant that is typically used to help clear the mind of the cobwebs brought on by fatigue — at least mental fatigue. But what is it that we use to help clear the spiritual dullness that sometimes comes into our lives as believers — in particular, as Reformed believers?

What follows are several "distinctive" elements of Reformed theology. They are distinctive not because Reformed thinkers are the only ones to embrace these ideas, they are distinctive because these are theological ideas essential to Reformed thinking and they are ideas that we get quite excited about. They are caffeine to our souls.

THE AUTHORITY OF SCRIPTURE

While we have already broached the subject of scriptural authority, I daresay that no other school of theology emphasizes the supremacy of the written word like that of Reformed Christianity.

The Reformed Christian's devotion to scripture has sometimes earned him the accusation of being a "bibliolater"[32] but this is hardly the case. It is not the book we worship, but the God of the book. Yet, the God we worship has condescended to show us the way and the truth and the life in a book, so we say, "Give us that book above all others and we will commit our lives to the God we cannot see by the word that we can read!"

When speaking of scriptural authority, the phrases "organic inspiration", "plenary verbal inspiration", "Biblical infallibility", and "Biblical inerrancy" tend to come up. These phrases frame how Reformed theologians have historically approached the matter of Biblical authority.

Organic inspiration refers to the process by which inspiration took place. Scripture is the word of God through the Prophets and Apostles, but not dictated in a mechanical way so as to obscure the personality of the author. God thus superintended the writing in such a way that the words and style the author he chose to use were exactly consistent with the will of God for his word. Thus Scripture is entirely the Word of God, yet we see the stylistic "fingerprint" of each author.

Plenary Verbal Inspiration means that God superintended not just the idea of scripture, but every word both great and small. Thus every word and every letter of the original manuscript is exactly what God willed it to be and could have been no other way. While human authors did pen the words, God is the one who created the personality and background of each author as well, thus governing what they stated completely.

Infallibility and Inerrancy derive their meaning from God's character. God is omniscient — he knows all things and he knows all things perfectly. Thus, when he relates that which he relates, they are related without error and without the possibility of error. And

---

[32] One who worships the Bible, thus making it into an idol.

this inerrancy applies not only to those major things to which the Bible speaks, but to all things — historical, economic, scientific, etc... Similarly, they cannot fail at what it is that they are meant to do — God's word will not return to him void.[33]

It is because of this view on Biblical authority that we can say along with the Apostle Paul, the scriptures are God-breathed and profitable to equip you for every good work.[34] It is also the reason that Reformed Christians place so much emphasis on expository preaching — declaration of and instruction in what God has said, not what man has imagined.

THE SOVEREIGNTY OF GOD

Many have summarized the Reformed view this way: "God saves sinners." It is God and God's work that brings salvation, thus he is sovereign not only in the ways and events of this world — even the smallest ones[35] — but he is absolutely sovereign over salvation.[36] We will talk at length about the doctrine of election later on in this book, but let it be said that God chose not only how he would save sinners but which sinners that he would save. From beginning to end, our salvation is the work of one — God alone.[37]

Some people feel a little uncomfortable with this doctrine of God's sovereignty in salvation the first time they are exposed to it. Again, we will come back to the idea later and develop it more fully from what the Bible teaches. For now, meditate on the analogy

---

[33] Isaiah 55:11.

[34] 2 Timothy 3:16-17.

[35] Proverbs 16:33; Isaiah 45:5-7.

[36] John 6:44; Romans 9:19-24.

[37] Theologians refer to this as "Divine Monergism" — the work of one, namely, God.

Paul uses in Romans 9:19-24 and what it means to be the clay in the potter's hands. Second, ask yourself this, would you rather have your salvation entrusted to your own care as a fallen person or to God's infinitely perfect care?

Only one can be sovereign and it is God and his will or man and his will — the Bible presents God as the sovereign one, not man, but we will come back to that idea later.

THE MAJESTY OF GOD

I fear that this is one element of our theology that seems to be lacking in much of the American church — even in Reformed circles. We have become so casual in our prayer life that we often forget into whose presence we are entering. The sacraments have often become so routine that we miss the sense that they are meant to transport us into the presence of the God of all creation. He is big and he is glorious and he is mighty and he has condescended to have a personal relationship with each believer. That reality ought to give us goose-bumps and make the small hairs on the back of our necks stand on end. It is a wonderful gift that God has given to us that we can enter into his presence, but we ought to regard it as a fearful one as well, much like the way that Isaiah and John responded to the presence of God. Isaiah's first response was to say, "woe is me!"[38] and John's was to fall down as if dead.[39]

Majesty deals with the impressiveness, the dignity, and the beauty that one carries by virtue of their person. And as for majesty, God surpasses all others to an infinite extent. It is this majestic nature of God that drives us to worship and it is this majestic nature of God as well, that finds unbelievers doubly guilty for their failure

---

[38] Isaiah 6:5.

[39] Revelation 1:17.

to worship. It is proper to give honor where honor is due — even the pagans and atheists recognize the merit of the artists, musicians, and performers in their midst. When a tradesman demonstrates the mastery of his trade in creating a masterpiece, whether through carpentry or through cookery, no one in their right mind would dare disrespect that craftsman by disparaging his work or attributing it to dumb luck. Yet, that is what the unbeliever does with respect to God and God is infinitely more of a craftsman and an artist than any human. Thus, their intentional disrespect is infinitely more damning.

THE CENTRALITY OF GRACE

It is by grace and by grace alone that we are saved! No human works contribute to or preserve our salvation — not even the smallest work lest grace become no longer grace.[40] Paul writes in Romans 9:14-16 that it is not the one who desires salvation nor is it the one who works toward salvation that brings about our saving — it is God in his mercy who gives salvation to his elect. In this passage, Paul links three participles in a row so it could be worded like this: not the one willing, not the one running, but God who is mercying.

And why is it that God would save us in this way? The answer is one that can fill books, but most basically because we cannot do anything on our own for all we do is tainted by sin. But Paul also ties grace to our human pride. He says that God has done this thing through grace so that no one would have any room to boast.[41] If salvation could be tied to anything that we might do — even to a decision that we make — then we have room to boast — and boast we will. Yet, when we understand that our salvation is a completely

---

[40] Romans 11:6.
[41] Ephesians 2:8-9.

God initiated and God worked event in our lives, our response is not to boast but to humbly praise and worship the one who has delivered us from the hell that we deserve.

Coram Deo

Nope, that is not a typo nor is it the name of a new line of automobiles. "Coram Deo" is a Latin phrase that means "before the face of God" or "in the presence of God. We understand that we live out all of our life in and before the presence of the Almighty God. He knows our every action and thus we ought to strive to live in a way that honors him not just in church, but in all of life.

We will come back to this idea further on when we discuss a Reformed perspective on Sanctification, but it is worth noting here that as God is Holy we too are called to be holy and live out our lives in a way that honors Him. In addition, even our vocations — whatever that may be, so long as it is a noble one — are to be practiced as if every piece of work we do is for the Lord's inspection. Just as the animal which had been presented at the temple in ancient Israel is totally committed to the sacrifice, we to are to be living sacrifices — totally committed — for the glory of Christ.[42]

Surely it can be said that Reformed theology encompasses more than those points listed above just as those in non-reformed contexts will also claim many of these elements. It is only in Reformed theology, though, that you find these elements not only coming together but being interwoven into the whole of the system of theology — and ever-present reminder to us that we are not God nor are our thoughts the word of God — thus we remember our place

---

[42] Romans 12:1.

is to worship, to submit our intellects to the revealed word, and to submit our wills to following the path of righteousness on which our God would have us tread. As goes the old Presbyterian hymn, "Trust and obey, for there's no other way, to be happy in Jesus, but to trust and obey."[43]

---

[43] Trust and Obey, written by John Sammis in 1887.

CHAPTER 7
THE ROOTS OF THE TULIP

The theology of Calvin is often summarized by the acronym: "TULIP," standing for Total Depravity, Unconditional Election, Limited Atonement, Irresistible Grace, and the Perseverance of the Saints. In the chapters that follow, we will explore these five theological ideas as they are presented to us in the scriptures. Yet, two things need to be noted up front — the first is that the five points of the TULIP do not exhaust Calvin's theology or his contributions to the Reformation and the second is that the ideas found in the TULIP are far older than Calvin and the debates around these ideas began long before Calvin's life. In addition, the TULIP itself was not articulated until 55 years after Calvin's death in the Synod of Dort.

Thus, if we are going to understand these doctrines, we first need to understand the roots of the debate that has surrounded these doctrines even today. And, if we are going to fairly discuss these doctrines with non-Reformed Christians, then we also need to understand the difference between Classic-Arminianism and John Wesley's Neo-Arminianism.

Augustine and Pelagius

While we would argue that the doctrines of the Reformed faith are found throughout scripture, there have been points of history marked by theological debate and sometimes outright heresy[44] that have surrounded the expression of these doctrines. Thus, we begin our trek through history in the fourth century AD.

Pelagius (354 — 420 AD) was an English monk and an aesetic.[45] On a pilgrimage that he made to Rome he encountered something that horrified him. The monks of his day were living in outright sin and immorality and did not seem to care. These monks had taken the attitude that since they were members of the church and ordained, given the pardon from the Bishop of Rome himself, they could live however they wanted. Pelagius' initial response was not unlike the response that I expect any evangelical Christian would give, and that is to cite the Apostle Paul's admonition against thinking that we ought to sin freely so that grace would abound all the more.[46]

Had Pelagius' response remained there, he might have gone down in history as an early church reformer. Yet, Pelagius did what so many people do when they see a group fall into error — he went to the other extreme (where he also ended up in error). Thus he added a theology of works into his theology of salvation. He reasoned that if God expects us to be perfect and holy, then we ought to have the capacity to do so. Logically, then, he continued, if we are

---

[44] The word "heresy" is often understood to mean: "error," though that betrays a misunderstanding of the term. Literally, the word heresy comes from the Greek word that means, "to divide." Thus, a heresy is a teaching that causes such a division — not between sects of Christianity — but causes a division where a person is clearly as not a part of the body of Christ — see the Apostle John's discussion of those heretics that he refers to as "Anti-Christs" — 1 John 2:18-25.

[45] One who forswears earthly comforts as a way to grow closer to God.

[46] Romans 6:1-2.

able to live up to the expectation and commands of God, then the effects of Original Sin must not be passed down from generation to generation.

Ultimately, Pelagius would take the view that the original sin of Adam and Eve only effected these first two parents. In addition, all children then have been born into the world morally neutral and thus learn sinful behavior from watching sinful adults. The coming of Jesus, then, was not so much about sacrifice as it was about modeling for us how to live a life that is honoring to God.

To address this matter, the church called on Augustine (354 - 430 AD), the Bishop of Hippo, to dispute Pelagius' ideas. Augustine demonstrated scripturally that the effects of original sin were passed down as well as the significance that Jesus' ministry and death on the cross was a sacrifice for our sins, not just a worthy model toward which we should strive.

Also, Augustine addressed Pelagius' view that if we "ought" to live a perfectly holy life, we "can" do so. Augustine drew from ancient forms and structure of logic to point out that "ought" does not imply "can." In the early 19th century, the Scottish philosopher, David Hume would essentially articulate the same principle, becoming known as "Hume's Guillotine." Today, we commonly refer to Pelagius' view (and similar errors) as committing the "moralistic fallacy." In other words, just because something ought to be so, does not mean that it can or ever will be so. The same works the other way around as well, just because something "is," that does not mean it "ought" to be so.[47]

Some historians argue that Pelagius recanted his beliefs; others say that he simply sought to placate the powers that be. Either way, he settled in Egypt and never returned to the world stage. But there were those who followed Pelagius with various adaptations of his views — this adaptation would eventually become known as

---

[47] This is called the "naturalistic fallacy."

"Semi-Pelagianism."

It should not be thought that the church's official position on the question was in any way undecided. Augustine's position was affirmed in 412AD by the Synod of Carthage, in 418 AD by the Council of Jerusalem, and in 431 AD by the Council of Ephesus. Nevertheless, seeds planted in soil of discontent do have a tendency to grow and that is what took place.

SEMI-PELAGIANISM

One must understand that the 5th Century was one of turmoil in Europe and the surrounding regions. The Germanic "Barbarians" were invading much of the land that was identified as Christian. This also then gave people with dissenting views the opportunity to spread them unchecked.

As mentioned before, there were many people sympathetic with Pelagius' view, though they sought to make it somewhat more orthodox and thus more presentable to the church as a whole. One ought not see Semi-Pelagianism as becoming the majority position at a specific point in time, rather see it as something that slowly began to emerge.

The Synod of Orange, held in 529 AD officially affirmed Augustinianism, yet in actuality, took a bit of a middle position, hoping to preserve the integrity of one church within this debate. Thus, Orange affirms the Doctrine of Original Sin as well as the reality that the Holy Spirit is the only one who can draw a man to Christ in salvation. At the same time, they rejected Augustine's view on Irresistible Grace and predestination to damnation. As we again move forward, by the end of the first millennium, Semi-Pelagianism had become the dominant position in the church and in the 13th Century would be articulated by no less a theological figure than

Thomas Aquinas.

By this time in history, the Semi-Pelagian view would accept that men are born in sin but reject that we are totally unable to do anything to contribute to our salvation, viewing man as spiritually sick but not spiritually dead. They affirmed that divine grace was needed to cling to Christ but that humans had to initiate this work and then God is seen as responding in assistance. Ultimately, one's eternal state rested in one's own will, not in the sovereign grace of God.

LUTHER AND ERASMUS

As the Medieval age gave way to the European Renaissance in the 14th and 15th centuries, Biblical scholarship began to change its approach and there was a renewed emphasis on the literal interpretation of the text in contrast to much of the spiritualism that marked Medieval thought. This, combined with the flood of ancient Greek manuscripts of the Bible that was flowing into Europe with the fall of the Byzantine Empire (1453 AD), brought about fertile soil not only for the Reformation, but for a resurgence in the debate over the relationship between God's sovereignty and the role of the human will.

For Reformed Christians, Desiderius Erasmus (1466-1536 AD) is a figure with whom we have a love/hate relationship. Erasmus was a strong critic of the abuses of the Roman Catholic church, but would never join with Luther in leaving the errant body.

Erasmus was quite prolific, but his most significant contribution to his age and to the Reformation was his publication of a Greek text to the New Testament taken from the many manuscripts and portions thereof that had been acquired as a result of the fall of Byzantium. In fact, in his lifetime, Erasmus would publish 5

New Testament texts, each time refining his work and approach. It is Erasmus' New Testament that Luther and Calvin would both end up using as they preached and laid forth doctrine during the Reformation.

Fourteen years Erasmus' junior, Martin Luther (1483-1546 AD) would end up engaging with Erasmus, partly in the hopes of gaining his allegiance in the Reformation. Luther would argue that Erasmus had built a theology that was essentially moralistic and not rooted in a Biblical understanding of grace. In fact, Luther even suggested that Erasmus read Augustine as Augustine was responsible for correcting Luther's own (as well as Calvin's) theological thinking.

Much more could be said about their debates, but what is most important for us at this stage is their debate around the nature of the human will. For Erasmus, a knowledge of the Truth (from scripture) yields the capacity to live it out — hence his moralism. Much as Augustine had countered Pelagius, Luther countered Erasmus by saying that knowledge of the Truth only creates obligation, not ability. Thus, as the Reformation spread throughout Europe and with the re-emphasis on Augustine's thought that came with it, the Augustinian/Semi-Pelagian debate was once again fresh in people's minds.

THE REMONSTRANCE

It seems kind of funny to jump right over John Calvin (1509 - 1564 AD) in a discussion of Calvinism, but there is a rhyme and reason for doing so at this stage. It should be noted, though, that because of John Calvin's zeal for the spread of the Gospel, Calvin's influence spread not only throughout Europe, but even as far as Brazil in the "New World." Thus, the branch of protestantism that found fertile soil in the Netherlands was dominantly Calvinistic in its approach to theology and Augustinian in its approach to the nature of the will with respect to God's sovereignty.

Nevertheless, there arose a Dutch theologian by the name of Jakob Hermanszoon (1560 - 1609 AD), better known today by his Latinized name: Jacob Arminius. In a series of debates with Franciscus Gomarus (1563 - 1641 AD), Arminius rejected the Calvinistic approach to predestination and began to develop his own answers, synthesizing elements of Pelagianism with Augustinianism. The year after Arminius' death, those students faithful to his teachings compiled them in a series of five points known as "The Remonstrance."[48] In 1610, these students of Arminius presented the Remonstrance to the church courts and the views of Arminius were formally debated. The five points set forth by the Remonstrance were as follows:

1. God elects only by foreseen faith: essentially the idea being set forth was that God does elect, but as God is outside of time and not bound by it, God looks down and foresees all who will choose to accept him by an act of their own free will. It is then those that choose God whom God elects — his election being a response to our decision to believe.

2. We are only partially depraved: this view is not a rejection of Original Sin so much as it is a rejection of the traditionally understood extent to which original sin affects the human. It was felt that sin warped humans, but that Jesus' atoning work on the cross redeemed the will of every human being so that humans are able to accept Christ if they so choose.

3. Grace is resistible: since the human will is able to choose, the final decision as to whom Grace extends is the individual

---

[48] "Remonstrance" simply means, "protest."

person's and God while God seeks to "woo" us to himself, we ultimately have the capacity to resist grace even unto death.

4. The effects of the Atonement are universal: the work of the cross is for all — the question belongs to each individual as to whether they would choose to receive it.

5. There is a possibility of falling away: as the human will is seen as sovereign in salvation, it is possible for the believer to fall away from faith and since grace is ultimately resistible, then it is possible for someone to enjoy the indwelling of the Holy Spirit for a season and then turn away.

THE SYNOD OF DORT (NOVEMEBER 1618 – MAY 1619)

To address the Remonstrance, a gathering of 93 pastors and theologians met and evaluated the scriptural support for every point that Arminius' followers presented. In addition to the preeminent theologians of the Netherlands, there were also representatives from Scotland, England, the German Palatinate, and Switzerland. Representatives from the French Huguenots were invited, but the pro-Roman Catholic government of the day forbade their attendance. The point of the matter is that this was not treated as a small regional dispute, but was formally investigated just as the Pelagian heresy had been investigated so many years before it.

After 6 months of meetings and debates, the Synod of Dort articulated a document containing five points, each one refuting one of the points of the Arminian Remonstrance and showing that Arminianism was heretical in its teaching. While originally written as a theological and judicial decision, the five points of the Synod of Dort became known as the Five Points of Calvinism, summarizing the basic doctrine of salvation contained within the Calvinistic school of thought. In the English speaking world, we use the acronymn, "TULIP," as mentioned earlier, to summarize these five points.

John Wesley (1703 - 1791 AD) and George Whitefield (1714 - 1770 AD)

Before we begin exploring each of the points of the Calvinistic TULIP, there is one more stop in the history books we must briefly make, and that is with the life of John Wesley. One might be tempted to say, "If the council of Dort demonstrated and condemned the views of Arminius as heretical, why didn't that end the debate?" Yet, to say that would be to close your eyes as to how fallen human nature works itself out in history. It seems that while some drift into error, others are always seeking novelty and maintaining a theological balance requires faithfulness to the scriptures and attentiveness to those things being taught in your midst.

John Wesley was a man zealous for the Gospel and for good works. Yet he struggled with the passive attitude that many of his contemporaries took toward the poor and those without the Gospel. Many of these pastors in the Anglican church had drifted into a practice called "hyper-calvinism."[49] In response to this error that Wesley recognized in practice around him, Wesley revived some of the teachings of Arminius and adapted them so they would not be outright heresy, but at the same time, left the spirit of human choice intact.[50]

---

[49] Hyper-calvinism is a heretical view that presumes that if God is going to save the elect, he will bring the elect to the church and thus no outreach or evangelism is necessary. The view is not consistent with Calvin's own missionary zeal and more importantly, it is not consistent with Jesus' great commission to go into the world and make disciples (Matthew 28:19).

[50] Wesley called his own position, "Neo-Arminianism" to distinguish it from classic Arminianism. It is worth noting this because it is common for Reformed

Wesley distinguished his "Neo-Arminianism" from Arminianism in three significant ways.

1. Wesley affirmed the doctrine of Original Sin and he recognized the effect of the fall on the generations that followed Adam and Eve.

2. Wesley affirmed the doctrine of Total Depravity, but with a nuance. He developed a theology of "Prevenient Grace,"[51] a view that the work of Christ's atonement gives all men the ability to choose faith in Christ when presented with the Gospel.

3. Wesley's view on whether or not grace is resistible was left undefined. When it came to Prevenient Grace, it was not resistible. When it came to Saving Grace, Wesley held to the Arminian stance that grace could be resisted even unto death. Then, when it comes to the believer, having chosen Christ, grace becomes irresistible in that God sovereignly leads his own. Even so, the believer can still lose their salvation, thus exchanging saving grace for wrath.

This final point in Wesley's theology demonstrates his desire to maintain the autonomy of the human will while at the same time not entirely disposing of God's sovereignty in his theology as Arminius had done. Yet, half-way compromises always lead to ambiguities and Wesley and Whitefield would have long debates regarding the matter. Augustus Toplady (1740 - 1778 AD) would also engage in this long debate along with Whitefield, trying to sway Wesley's view

---

scholars to mistake this and refer to Wesley as Arminian, for he was not. He was technically a Neo-Arminian just as are those who have followed Wesley's theological model.

[51] Prevenient Grace means, "the Grace that goes before." It is spoken of as "before" in that this grace goes out before people make a "choice" to accept the Gospel.

back to orthodox Calvinism, though unsuccessfully.[52]

It is often asked why, after 1,300 years of debate and theologians demonstrating the error of the Pelagian/Semi-Pelagian/Arminian view, why Wesley's Neo-Arminianism took hold and spread throughout much of the world. In fact, it can be fairly said that the majority of professing Christians in the world today hold to a view that has descended from Wesley's Neo-Arminianism. Certainly, something can be said about Wesley's ability to mobilize people and promote his ideas, but I think that the answer has more to do with the historical context in which Wesley and his contemporaries were living.

In the 1600s, philosophical rationalism began to dominate the world of thought. Thinkers like Baruch Spinoza (1632 - 1677 AD), Gottfried Leibniz (1646 - 1716 AD), and Immanuel Kant (1724 - 1804 AD) promoted the idea of the supremacy of the human reason to solve any and all problems of life. With this emphasis on human reason and the human will, it seems that Wesley's Neo-Arminianism was a natural child of the 18th century enlightenment.

---

[52] It should be noted that the debates between the Wesleys on one side and Toplady and Whitefield on the other got quite heated at points, though by the end of their lives, these men had reconciled in faith even if not in theology. Wesley would even preach Whitefield's memorial service back in England.

CHAPTER 8
THE BUS AND THE LIMO

The historical debate ultimately revolves around the relationship between the Human and the Divine wills — "Which will ultimately win out?", would be another way to put it. There is an analogy that I have often related, meant to contrast the difference between a Calvinistic and a Wesleyan/Neo-Arminian perspective on the nature of the will. As with all analogies, it breaks down fairly easily if pressed and it certainly has its weaknesses. Yet, this analogy has stuck with me, not so much because of its great theological precision, but because of its source, for I originally heard this analogy from a Methodist professor as an explanation for why the Wesleyan view is better than the Calvinistic view of the will. I will allow you to be the judge as to which paradigm is more appealing, let alone, more Biblical.

The analogy goes as follows: From the Wesleyan perspective, salvation is represented by a large bus upon which those who are saved will ride. Jesus is the bus driver and not only pilots the bus toward potential passengers, but also opens the door to the bus and bids people to come on board. Yet, he never leaves his driver's seat, relying on his word and the will of the person hearing his word, giving the person the ultimate choice as to whether he steps onto the bus or not. Once on the bus, the passengers have the limitless bliss of being able to ride the bus of salvation, knowing that they are on that bus, but at every stop they have the opportunity to get back off the bus if they choose. When they die, whether they are still on the bus or off the bus determines their eternal destination: heaven or hell.

The analogy continues to describe the Calvinistic view in this way: salvation is now represented by a gangster's limousine. Again, Jesus is driving, and when he sees someone on the street that he chooses, he pulls over, the doors swing open, several mobsters jump out (the Holy Spirit), whack the person over the head, drag him into the limousine, and don't let him out until you are dead and thus in heaven.

Okay, the analogy is a poor one, though we might snicker at the mental image of Jesus being a gangster grabbing the elect one by one into his limo. At the same time, the analogy does portray the role of the human will in both theological schools. The Wesleyan school emphasizes the will to such an extent that Jesus' hands are tied — he can do nothing that would violate the will of the person — even to the point of allowing them to go into eternal damnation. In contrast, Calvinists recognize God's will as sovereign over the will of a person, though perhaps the analogy of whacking someone over the head and dragging them into a limo is a bit extreme.[53]

---

[53] Yet, it should be noted that in John 6:44, Jesus makes the statement that it is impossible for someone to come to him in faith unless the Father first draws him. That word for "draw" is the Greek word, ἕλκω (elko), which describes the action of dragging something that has no ability to move itself. It was also often used to describe how a farmer might put a rope on a stubborn donkey's head and pull the animal along quite against its will. Such was the word that Jesus chose to describe the Father's "drawing" or "dragging" of us to his Son against our fallen will — not too far from being dragged into a limousine...

The Freedom of the Will

The question that must be raised as we look at these two systems of thought is just how free the human will is — or perhaps a better way of wording it is, what does it mean for the human will to be free?

There are essentially four philosophical positions that one might hold when it comes to the freedom of the will — two of these positions are extreme positions and would be heretical positions to hold. The other two represent positions held within orthodox Christianity, one being a Calvinistic position and the other being a Wesleyan one.

Extremes

The two extremes are that of absolute determinism (a form of fatalism) and that of absolute libertarian freedom. The first agues that as God is sovereign, we are nothing more than robots moving through life, more or less as passive observers. We perceive ourselves to be making decisions and acting, but that perception is little more than a farce — an optical illusion of sorts. There is a will, but that will is not an individual will located in the person, but is instead a universal will drawing us along a pathway toward destruction.[54]

Spinoza[55] illustrated this idea of absolute determinism by describing a rock that was thrown and given consciousness mid-flight. His argument was that the rock would perceive himself as

---

[54] The Greek idea of the "Fates" is embraced here, that all our choices are ultimately nothing more than means to the ends determined by the Fates.

[55] Baruch Spinoza (1632-1677), was a Dutch philosopher of Jewish heritage who was foundational in developing a foundation for the rationalism and enlightenment that would follow in the 18th century as well as for liberal Biblical Criticism.

flying of his own power and will.[56] Schopenhauer[57] took Spinoza's argument further by arguing that if the stone perceived itself to be flying of its own will, it would be correct in doing so because perception dictates reality.

The great problem with absolute determinism from a Christian perspective should be obvious — where there is no genuine will, one cannot be held responsible for one's own sins. Yet, scripture is quite clear that our sins are real and we are held responsible for them in God's eyes.[58] Thus, this position of the will needs to be rejected outright.

The second extreme position that must be rejected is that of absolute libertarian freedom. This views man's will as absolute and that every decision he makes as being perfectly free and uninfluenced by outside designs. Such is the view of Deism[59] as well as that of Open Theism.[60] The obvious error of this view lies in the view of God, limiting his work by our wills and making his sovereignty little more than high hopes for his people.

---

[56] Spinoza, Epistle 62.

[57] Arthur Schopenhauer (1788-1860), was a German philosopher, who combined elements of Bhuddism with atheism and was a significant influence on later philosophers like Nietzsche, Freud, and Jung.

[58] See Leviticus 16:20-22; Deuteronomy 27:1; Micah 6:8; Malachi 4:4; Matthew 5:19-20, 7:12; James 2:10; Revelation 20:13.

[59] A philosophy that acknowledges the presence of a God who created all things, set them into motion, and then took a step back as a passive observer in the events of history. God is seen as so transcendent that he is unable or unwilling to enter into fallen reality — a view that has its roots back in the flesh/spirit dichotomy of Gnosticism and Greek Philosophy (spirit being pure and physical being defiled).

[60] Open Theism is the position that God is an actor in the drama of history but that he does not know the future — the best that he can do is to work along with his people to bring about what is best for them. This perspective limits not only God's knowledge but also his power and even prophesy is nothing more than a "best guess" on God's part. History becomes a collaboration between God and man as events get worked out.

ORTHODOX PERSPECTIVES[61]

Within Christian orthodoxy there are two broad views regarding the human will where people fall — one Wesleyan and one Cavinistic. The Wesleyan (or Neo-Arminian) view would hold to a limited form of Libertarian freedom. This view holds that God is sovereign in the governance of his universe, yet has chosen to restrict his own sovereignty to allow people freedom of the will when it comes to salvation (the bus in the analogy above). This view sees God's self-restriction of his sovereignty as a restriction of the outworking of his power, not a restriction of his potential power (he could override our wills, but actively chooses not to).

From a Reformed position, though, the limited libertarian freedom of the Neo-Arminian camp is not faithful to scripture. Often we find God superintending the will of individuals like Pharaoh[62], false prophets[63], Balaam[64], and Lydia.[65] Even Solomon recognized that unless it is God who would incline the people's heart toward faithfulness, they would fall into sin.[66] Also, during Hezekiah's reign, it was God who inclined the hearts of the people to himself so that they would do what the king was commanding them to do.[67] David recognizes as well his own inability to change his own heart, thus in his prayer of repentance, asks God to "create in me a clean

---

[61] It should be noted that while the Wesleyan/Neo-Arminian view is unhelpful in understanding the outworking of God's sovereignty, it is not heretical and stays within the parameters of scripture (at least from a certain perspective).

[62] Exodus 10:20.

[63] 1 Kings 22:22.

[64] Numbers 23:5.

[65] Acts 16:14. Note that this passage alone is one of the most significant passages regarding the nature of belief as well as the nature of the will — we will return to Lydia in more depth in future chapters.

[66] 1 Kings 8:56-61.

[67] 2 Chronicles 30:12.

heart."⁶⁸ Furthermore, the very presence of prophesy inclines one to a description of a God who can not only predict events of the future by foreknowledge⁶⁹ but of a God who so ordains them according to the council of his own will.⁷⁰

Thus, the Reformed position is what typically is called Compatiblism or "Compatiblistic Freedom of the Will." This view argues that we act in accordance with our wills, choosing to do what we most desire to do at that moment, but since God has designed our wills and our personalities as well as the events surrounding us in the world, all of our choices are consistent with God's design — even if I choose to sin. Thus Paul can say that God has caused us to will and to work for his good pleasure.⁷¹

Some have balked at this view, believing it to make God the author of our sins. Yet, while God permits our sinful behavior, it is we who sin, not God, and thus it is we who are guilty of those sins. Ultimately, though, it is God who has permitted sin to take place in this world of ours.⁷² He is sovereign over all things, yet we make

---

⁶⁸ Psalm 51:10. We should also note that the term "create" used here is the Hebrew word בָּרָא (bara), which when applied to God, typically means to create out of nothing by divine fiat. While we will discuss both Justification and Sanctification later in this book in the chapter on the Ordo Salutis, it should be noted that this verse places both ideas side by side. God is to create a clean heart (a singular act of divine creation — regeneration and justification) but renew a right spirit within me (ongoing sanctification).

⁶⁹ Looking out across the spectrum of time to see what will happen.

⁷⁰ Ephesians 1:11.

⁷¹ Philippians 2:13.

⁷² Some have raised the question as to why a God who is sovereign over the will of men would allow sin to take place. The answer given by Augustine seems to be about the best — without our sin we would not know the fullness of Christ's sacrificial love for us. As much misery as has been brought into the world as a result of sin, that misery cannot match the immense depth of love of a God who would enter into our miserable world in the flesh, experience life as we live it, and then die a sacrificial death on our behalf, having committed no sin of his own. That notion in and of itself ought to drive us to adore and worship.

decisions and actions that are free while consistent with our design.

Compatiblism is often illustrated with the idea of the heart. When we are born in sin into this world we are born with a heart of stone and in our being born again, God replaces our stone heart with a heart of flesh.[73] Yet, this "heart transplant" operation does not take place all at once. So long as we walk in this world, we live as those who are torn, pulled toward sin but desiring to please God, as Paul wrote, "the things that I want to do I don't do and the things that I don't want to do, I do!"[74] This reflects the tension within the life of the believer. The heart of stone wishes to beat for nothing but sin and thus is cold and dead. The heart of flesh wishes to beat for God and for God alone. As an unbeliever this tension did not exist, but for the believer, we exist in tension, seeking to put that old heart to death and live in a way consistent with the new heart. In theological terms, we call this process, sanctification.

The picture that is had here is that of God putting the heart of flesh into our being right next to the heart of stone and then slowly chiseling away at the heart of stone, breaking it into bits, until we are in glory with him and the stone is entirely gone from our being. Thus, as we live and mature in faith, that wrestling match also ought to grow easier as we long more and more for the things of God and hate the sins of this world more and more.

The Apostle Paul applies this idea by speaking of the circumcision of the heart.[75] The idea of the heart's circumcision is nothing new as it is found in the Old Testament scriptures as well[76], but he uses the language to point out that it is one's heart circumcision, not one's fleshly circumcision, that identifies one as a believer in Jesus Christ and thus as a member of the body of the

---

[73] Ezekiel 36:26.

[74] Romans 7:18-24.

[75] Romans 2:28-29.

[76] Deuteronomy 10:16; 30:6.

people whom God has blessed — the true Jew being the one who is spiritually circumcised. Some of suggested this idea of circumcision lends itself to a picture of one heart that has been calcified and coated with stone and the process of circumcision being one of chiseling that stone away.[77] Though a slightly different analogy than that of having two hearts, the same idea is captured in that there is tension between the heart of flesh and the heart of stone.

ST. AUGUSTINE AND BOSTON... NOT JUST TWO CITIES...

To explain this idea of the heart, Augustine developed a 3-fold model to describe the relationship of man's will toward sin. By the time of Thomas Boston[78], this view had been expanded into a 4-fold division as presented briefly below:

1. In the man's "Pre-Fallen" state, Adam and Eve were morally neutral, able to choose sin or to choose righteousness. This state was lost when they fell in the garden.[79]
2. In man's "Post-Fallen" state, man is only able to sin. All of mankind, after Adam and Eve, is born into this state.[80]
3. In man's "Post-Fallen and Post-Conversion" state, one is able to sin and able to resist sin, though resistance of sin is only possible in Christ. This state is different than the state

---

[77] The psalmist also speaks of the heart of the unbeliever as being coated in a thick layer of fat, thus making it unfeeling and insensitive to the Law of God (Psalm 119:70).

[78] Thomas Boston (1676-1732) was a minister and leader amongst the Scottish Covenanters known for his staunch defense of Calvinism.

[79] Theologians use the Latin phrase "posse peccare; posse non-peccare" (able to sin; able not to sin) to abbreviate this state.

[80] Abbreviated by the Latin phrase: "non-posse non-peccare."

of Adam and Eve in that we are still fallen and thus still drawn toward sin, but by the power of the Holy Spirit and to the glory of God, sin is sometimes resisted to God's glory alone.[81]

4. In man's "State of Glory," he will not be able to sin any longer.[82]

Freedom and Glory

It should be noted that in glory those who are believers will be purged of their sin nature and not only will never be drawn to sin, but the entire possibility of sinning will be removed. This is one more argument against the Neo-Arminian position that the potential for sinning is necessary to have human freedom of the will. It should be argued that it is in heaven when the will will most truly be free — sin and its possibility bind the will — and thus the argument about freedom needing the possibility of sin is nonsensical.

---

[81] Abbreviated by the Latin phrase: "posse peccare; posse non-peccare en Christo."

[82] Abbreviated by the Latin phrase: "non-posse peccare."

CHAPTER 9
TOTAL DEPRAVITY

What a cheery way this is to start out the Tulip. Nevertheless, such is our state after the Fall. It should be noted that there is often confusion as to what this doctrine teaches and what it does not teach. To begin with, the doctrine of Total Depravity *does not* mean that we are as bad, sinful, or wicked as we possibly can be. Such a position would be easy to disprove were one only to open the newspaper and read articles of violence alongside of articles about heroic service or a rescue. The bottom line is that some people (at least on human terms) are worse than others. More importantly, no matter how wicked a person is on this earth, he could always be more wicked and those who leave this earth without repenting of their sins and turning to Jesus Christ as their Lord and Savior will one day truly know what it means to be as wicked and evil as they possibly can be — that is, in the torments of hell.

A discussion of Total Depravity deals with both our state of being and our potential for sin apart from a divine change being worked upon us. What Total Depravity means is that every part of our person, from our flesh to our personality, from our mind to our will to our passions, is affected by sin. There is not any part of us, not even the smallest bit, that is unaffected by sin.

Thus, our state of being is wretched and helpless[83], but that is not the worst of it. Our Total Depravity is also joined by a Total Inability to do anything to change or improve our state. In the western world, so called "self-help" books are all the rage. People buy these books to change their habits, lose weight, make themselves more productive, or otherwise feel better about themselves. Yet, when it comes to our spiritual life and righteousness, we can not ever do anything to please God and improve our standing before him.[84] All we do is sin. We cannot even acknowledge Jesus as the Messiah apart from the work of the Holy Spirit upon us.[85] The Apostle Paul writes that in and of themselves, no one is righteous and no one genuinely seeks after God.[86] We all start into this fallen world in an equally wretched state — to quote Augustine: non-posse non-peccare.[87]

Original Sin

So, how did we find ourselves in such a wretched state? The answer to that question originates all of the way back in creation. God had made a perfect world and in that perfect world he placed a garden — a paradise in which he placed the first man and woman. In this garden, God gave his first people both instructions and prohibitions.

As instructions, God commanded them to "work" and to "keep" the garden.[88] The first of those words focuses on the

---

[83] Romans 7:18; Philippians 3:8; Isaiah 64:6. In Philippians, the Apostle Paul is equating his own works to dung, that which is defiled and fit only for burning. Isaiah similarly compares his works to a menstrual rag used by women, again to be burned afterwards.

[84] Romans 3:3:20.

[85] Matthew 16:17.

[86] Romans 3:10-11

[87] Not possible not to sin. See chapter 8.

[88] Genesis 2:15.

cultivation of the plants that God had put into his paradise. The second of those words focuses on the fact that they were to protect what God had established, keeping it free from sin and defilement. Interestingly enough, when these words are found together in the Hebrew language, they are always found in a context of worship, implying that this act of working and keeping was part of the worship of our first parents.

In doing so, they were also instructed to fill the world with their kind, taking dominion over the natural order.[89] Humans were to be God's representatives in the world, ordering it and governing it in a way that would honor their great God and King. This was the environment into which our first parents were placed — and a state which our first parents would lose.

There was also a prohibition. While they were permitted to eat of the fruit of the trees of the garden, they were commanded not to eat the fruit of one particular tree in the midst of the garden — the tree of the knowledge of good and evil.[90] In fact, they were expressly commanded that if they did eat of that tree they would surely die.[91] One point that should be noted about this tree is that Adam and Eve, in the garden and in relationship with God, did understand the nature of goodness, it was evil that they did not understand along with the chasm of disparity between the two — such is what their disobedience would bring.

Of course, most of us know the Genesis 3 account well. Satan, the serpent[92], tests Eve's knowledge of God's prohibition and her willingness to be in obedience to that prohibition. Eve's knowledge

---

[89] Genesis 1:28.

[90] Genesis 2:16-17.

[91] In Hebrew, the phrase is emphatic: "You will die-die" or perhaps, "You will be killed dead." There is nothing ambiguous about the punishment offered for this sin.

[92] Genesis 3:1; Revelation 12:9.

of the prohibition is clearly flawed as she both adds to and subtracts from the commandment of God. She adds that they are not allowed to touch the fruit of the tree and she reduces the emphatic nature of the punishment — "you will die." Satan does what Satan does best, and capitalized on her error, twisting the truth of God and accusing God of being a lier.[93] Ultimately, Eve was forced to make a choice — was God lying or was Satan lying? Sadly, by her action, she accused God of lying as did her husband, Adam, who was with her.[94]

The judgment would follow. Adam and Eve did die on that day, though not physically, instead they died spiritually. They also began the process of dying physically on that day. In addition, they were removed from the garden and the whole of the created order fell along with them (they had dominion over the earth, so the earth suffered as they suffered). In fact, the created order suffered the brunt of the curse for God never curses those people he plans to redeem.[95] No longer would Adam or the children of Adam live in paradise.[96]

There is one glimmer of light in the whole account of mankind's fall, and that is in the form of a promise. In Genesis 3:15, God foretells of one who is of the seed of the woman who will come and crush the head of the serpent, but doing so at a personal cost (his heel would be crushed). This, of course, will be fulfilled by Jesus himself and the early church fathers were so moved by this promise that they referred to it as the "proto-evangelion" or "the first Gospel." Adam and Eve would never lay down their heads to go to

---

[93] Genesis 3:4-5.

[94] Genesis 3:6.

[95] Genesis 3:17 — "cursed is the ground because of you" — this is a form of substitution, the earth taking man's punishment and is a foreshadowing of the substitution that would be worked by God's Son, Jesus Christ, as he bore the guilt of our sins on the cross.

[96] Note: children under the headship of their Father will suffer alongside of their father for his sins.

sleep at night without the promise of a coming savior — and it is into this promise that the Old Testament saints put their faith.

THE TRANSMISSION OF ORIGINAL SIN

As Children of Adam and Eve, every person on the planet has inherited the guilt of their sin. As noted above, Adam was our Federal head, and thus we also pay the penalty for his sin. God makes this principle clear not only by leaving the Garden of Eden perpetually barred[97], never allowing a new generation to return, but that he punishes the sins of those who hate him for three and four generations.[98] Interestingly, in Jesus' parable of the unforgiving servant[99], Jesus uses the illustration of a steward who owed his master 10,000 talents. Not only was this a sum larger than any of Jesus' contemporaries could have imagined, it was also a sum that could only have been accrued by generations of bad management of the master's money — a debt handed down from father to son for generation after generation...

Sometimes people think that this view of Federal Headship is "unfair" of God. "Why can't I be judged on my own merits alone?", people say. Yet, when rightly understood, Federal Headship is a wonderful doctrine, for were we to be judged on our own merits alone, sinners as we are, we would still fall short of God's expectation and face the righteous punishment for our sins. Instead, through faith in Jesus Christ, Jesus becomes our new Federal Head, and thus is referred to as "the Second Adam" by the Apostle Paul[100],

---

[97] Genesis 3:23-24.

[98] Exodus 20:5-6, 34:7-14; Deuteronomy 5:9, 28:18; Jeremiah 32:18; Matthew 23:34-36.

[99] Matthew 18:23-35.

[100] Romans 5:12-21.

and thus we are judged on the basis of Christ's righteousness, not our own nor our first father's. Unfair, perhaps in the sense that we are also given in Christ what we did not earn ourselves — but I don't know of one believer who would exchange what was given to him or her in Christ for what he or she truly deserves.

Theologians have also argued that there may be a biological component to original sin. This is based on the language of Genesis 5:3, where Seth is described as being in the likeness of Adam — a likeness marred by sin. Further, those who would argue for this component would also cite trends within a family for children to share some of the sinful tendencies of their parents — even in those cases where children are separated from their parents at birth (adoptions, for example). While this line of reasoning is based on some speculation, it should be noted that certain characteristics and tendencies toward sin do seem to pass down from parents to children.

ACTUAL SIN

As if the guilt of Adam's sin passed down to us is not significant enough, because of Adam's fall, we have lost our original righteousness and thus are not able to resist sin and please God apart from Christ working in us. And, that bent toward sins means that we add sins of our own doing to the guilt we bear. These sins are both sins of thought and action as well as sins of commission and omission. We are doubly condemned. But what is sin?

The Hebrew word that is translated as sin in the Old Testament is derived from the verb חָטָא (chata'), which means, "to miss the mark." In principle, it is an archery term meant to describe one missing the bullseye when taking aim at a target. Thus, Biblically, our sin is missing the mark set for us by God himself in both our disposition and in our actions. And what is that mark? Perfection.[101] Thus, on our own, we never make the mark.

The Heidelberg Catechism takes the question one step further. It poses the question as to what sin is and it states that sin is hatred toward God.[102] One can easily see this connection, for if one shows love to God through obedience,[103] then disobedience must in turn be an expression of contempt and hatred. Granted, this is language that many of us would feel uncomfortable with, but that is because many of us have a fairly low view of sin. We tend to think of sin in the terms of the mischief of a child that is easily overlooked and forgiven. Yet, Biblically, sin is outright rebellion against God. It is Adam and Eve accusing the God of Truth[104] of being a liar[105] while believing the Father of Lies.[106] Sin is lawlessness.[107] And of this sin, all mankind is guilty.

It is without question that until a person understands the gravity of their sin they will never understand the greatness of the salvation that is offered in Jesus Christ. We are not just spiritually sick in our sins as the Neo-Arminian would argue, but we are dead in our trespasses.[108] Yet, that truth is good news. For as sin reigns in death, God permits it so that grace may reign through the righteousness of Christ.[109] We can take no credit for our salvation — it is all of grace, from beginning to end, grace abounds despite our

---

[101] Matthew 5:48.

[102] Heidelberg Catechism, Question 5: "Can you live up to all of this perfectly?" Answer: "No, I have a tendency to hate God and my neighbor."

[103] John 14:15.

[104] Isaiah 65:16.

[105] When they questioned the truthfulness of God's statement, "You shall surely die," they were in essence saying, "No, I think that God is lying to us…"

[106] John 8:44.

[107] 1 John 3:4.

[108] Ephesians 2:1.

[109] Romans 5:21.

death.[110]

DOES THIS MAKE A DIFFERENCE?

If the idea that this is important — really important — has not yet registered, let me emphasize its significance. When you understand the horrors of our sin, it helps us to appreciate the wonders of grace. We did not deserve it and could never merit it, but God offers it anyway. We are wretched in our sin, yet Christ died for us…despite ourselves.

This is the universal condition of mankind, which gives confidence to the missionary message — we have an answer to the question that has been haunting the nations — what do I do with my sinful self? Regardless of race or skin-color or geography, the Gospel has the universal answer to the universal problem of sin that all who come to Christ in faith will live. That makes a big difference as it means we are without excuse when it comes to sharing our faith.

---

[110] Romans 5:8.

Chapter 10
Unconditional Election

The idea of election is common in scripture, though it is often one that makes people uncomfortable. The doctrine itself simply states that before the foundation of the world, God chose a group of people from across the timeline to give new life to and to redeem from their sins for his own glory. That election is not based on anything but grace, it is not based on anything within those whom God elected.

Both the Wesleyan groups and the Calvinistic groups affirm the idea of election, though the explanations of the doctrine are very different. Wesley, like Arminius before him, took a view popularized by the Roman philosopher, Boethius.[111] Boethius argued that God, being outside of time, saw the entirety of the timeline at once and thus, his election was a matter of foresight and not a matter of foreordination. This view has reigned popular in many circles because it allows for a God who elects but also allows for absolute free will (God only elects those who he foresees will come to him in

---

[111] Anicius Manlius Severinus Boethius (480-525 AD) is considered by many to be the last of the Roman philosophers and the philosophical bridge into Medieval philosophy. It has been argued by some that Boethius was a Christian, though the argument is speculative at best.

faith).

There is a second view that seems to have arisen within Wesleyan circles which argues that Christ is the only elect one from before the foundations of the earth[112] and we find our election in Christ — an election gained through choosing Christ in faith. Apart from being a very poor interpretation of Ephesians 1:4, it also makes God quite oblivious as to who will and will not come to him.

Biblically, the Reformed understanding of Election is the one to be held. It is God who elects and he elects entirely as a matter of grace and not our works, doing so from before the foundation of the earth as part of God's eternal decree. And all of this is not because of foresight or our choice — but it is to reveal his glory to mankind.

A Choice is Made

In the Greek New Testament, there are three words that reflect the idea of election: ἐκλέγομαι, ἐκλεκτός, and ἐκλογή. These words are found a combined total of 48 times in the New Testament writings and where used, they reflect not only a choice, but a choice of specific people or ideas, not a generic body of people. For example, Jesus elected 12 Apostles[113] and God elected to set Paul apart for Apostleship.[114]

The plainest use of the term is found in Romans 9:11. In context, Paul is speaking about how from the beginning of the Jewish people, God even chose from amongst the children of Abraham to work and thus, just because one can biologically trace their lineage back to Abraham does not mean that they are part of

---

[112] Ephesians 1:4.

[113] Luke 6:13.

[114] Galatians 1:5; 1 Corinthians 1:1.

the covenant. Instead, it is those who have faith in God who are part of the covenant.[115] Paul continues this line of argumentation by pointing out that God continued this practice of election by electing Jacob over Esau before they were even born — before either could do anything good or bad to otherwise earn God's favor.[116] Paul continues that this has been done so that "God's purpose of election might be established."[117] Paul continues with the passage of scripture that often makes people uncomfortable — "Just as it is written, for Jacob have I loved but Esau have I hated."

Paul anticipates the objection that we might raise — "is this unjust of God?" And Paul says, "no." God is God and as God he has the right to have mercy and compassion on those whom he wishes to show mercy and compassion.[118] Paul then uses two examples to illustrate his point, the first from history and the second by way of analogy.

The first example is that of Pharaoh[119], whom God raised up to power only for the purpose of showing his great power by crushing him down. The second is an analogy of a potter who is making clay vessels.[120] Paul goes on to say that it is the potter's absolute right, as master over the clay, to make some vessels for honored use and other vessels for dishonorable use — even to make some vessels for destruction. Does anyone feel sorry for the clay pigeons that are flung into the air and shot at by sportsmen? Of course not, they were made for destruction — so too are those whom God has not elected to bring to himself.

Thinking of God in this light often makes people a bit weak

---

[115] Romans 9:7-8.
[116] Romans 9:10-12.
[117] Romans 9:11.
[118] Romans 9:15; Exodus 33:19.
[119] Romans 9:17-18.
[120] Romans 9:19-21.

in the knees — and perhaps it should. God is author and master over all creation, maker of all things, and judge of all men. As we have already discussed, we all deserve wrath — it is the compassion and mercy that God shows to some that makes the exception to the rule. Paul even addresses those who would be uncomfortable in thinking of God in these terms by saying, "what if God chose to be patient with the great wickedness of men for the purposes of making his glory known in its fullness?" In other words, God is allowing wickedness to run its course in this world to do two things — first to demonstrate his awesome grace by redeeming a remnant of humanity to himself by grace (not by anything in those whom he saves) and second, to show his great might by ultimately destroying those wicked ones who would raise their fist in rebellion against him at the height of their power and might.[121]

And, just to make sure we understand the election of God, Paul inserts in the middle of this exposition the reminder that election depends not on the will of men nor on the labors of men. It depends on the mercy of God. One might respond, why doesn't God just elect everyone to salvation? Wouldn't that make him even more merciful? Again, when we enter down this road of thinking, we neglect the language of the potter and the clay, but let me also propose that were God to elect all then he would not be electing any, for election is a choice of one from another and if all are chosen no choice is really being made. It makes the idea nonsensical.

FOREKNOWING AND FOREORDAINING

Neo-Arminians would still assert that this kind of election could be based on God's foreknowledge and not God's foreordination, essentially arguing that God's foreordination is based on but separate

---
[121] Romans 9:22-24.

from his foreknowledge while the Calvinist would argue that the two are intertwined in their meaning. If foreordination is simply a result of foreknowledge, God cannot be said to ordain anything, only to look over the horizon of time and then state what he sees taking place.

Imagine a person, let's call him, Jack, building a time machine so that he can see what is going to happen in the near future — a kind of mechanical crystal ball of sorts. Jack witnesses that a certain horse is going to win a race, at long odds, and then bets on that horse. Perchance, let us say that Jack has several friends that are close to him who don't know about the machine Jack has built, but trust his instincts. So, he tells them to bet on this certain horse so that they can win money as well. Now, in this case, can it ever be said that Jack has ordained that a certain horse will win the race? Obviously not, and if he states to others that he has ordained his horse to win, he would be a great liar and a fraud. It must be similarly so with God; if his foreordination is purely based on foreknowing what will take place, then he is genuinely ordaining nothing. Such is the great flaw in the Neo-Arminian perspective.[122]

The best place to illustrate the relationship between foreknowing and foreordaining is found in Romans 8:29. Here, within this verse, both terms are found practically side by side. It begins

---

[122] There are some who would take this idea of foreknowing and foreordaining further than we have discussed here. They would argue that not only does God know what will happen, he knows all the eventualities of every decision we make, so he knows what potentially could happen were other decisions made. In this line of thought, then, the Neo-Arminian argues that God ordains the line of events that leads us to make certain decisions, but does not ordain the decisions we will make. In some way, this is meant as a sort of half-way compromise, yet this still puts too much weight on foreknowledge and at best makes God a predictor of what could or probably will happen, but not of what will happen with surety — which is the way that the Bible presents God when he tells us what will happen even to the extent of hardening Pharaoh's heart to bring it about.

with the phrase: "For those he foreknew[123] he also predestined[124]...". This passage is the beginning of what William Perkins[125] called "the Golden Chain."[126] Here Paul ties together these ideas making them inseparable, but the debate remains as to which is primary. Yet, as has already been mentioned, if foreordaining is based simply on foreknowledge, it cannot be genuinely said to be ordaining at all — only a revealing of what will take place.

Furthermore, we must raise the question as to how the Apostle Paul understood the idea of knowledge in the first place, for the Hebrew understanding of "knowing" implied not just simply observational knowledge but also implied a relationship with that which was known.[127] Thus, from Paul's perspective, the idea of foreknowing implies a relationship that exists from before the foundation of the world. Thus, God can say to Jeremiah that, "Before I formed you in the womb, I knew you...".[128] Similarly, Paul relates that he was set apart for the work of Apostleship before he was born.[129] Even Peter states that the coming of Christ was "foreknown" before the foundation of the world and revealed in these last times for our sake[130] — all the while recognizing that the

---

[123] The term here is προγίνωσκω (proginosko), meaning "to know beforehand."

[124] The term here is προορίζω (pro'oridzw), meaning "to decide upon before hand — to predetermine or foreordain."

[125] William Perkins (1558-1602) was one of the leaders of the Puritan movement in his era and was one of the early puritan divines to begin publishing books for the layman, not just for the scholarly theologians of his day.

[126] Those God foreknew he also predestined and those he predestined he called, justified, and glorified. There are no loose links in the chain — it is an assurance that the good work God begins in a believer he will bring to completion in glory — Philippians 1:6.

[127] Thus it can be said that Adam "knew" his wife and she became pregnant. Genesis 4:1.

[128] Jeremiah 1:5.

[129] Galatians 1:15.

[130] 1 Peter 1:20.

coming of Christ was something that God had ordained — it was intentionally chosen, not just foreseen.[131] Thus foreknowledge must be based on fore-ordination, not the other way around.

Omnipotence of God

When speaking of foreordination, it is appropriate to bring into the discussion the question of God's ability to bring about those things that he decrees. Omnipotence is the theological term that we use to describe God's ability to bring to be all that he sets forth to bring in to being.[132] Thus, it should be stated that when God so decrees something to take place, it follows that such a thing will take place as God has the ability to make it so. Thus, Peter can say in his sermon at Pentecost, that it was due to the definite plan[133] as well as the foreknowledge of God.[134] Similarly, Luke writes of Paul and Barnabas' preaching in Antioch of Pisidia that when the Gentiles heard the preaching, all those who were decreed for eternal life believed.[135]

---

[131] In fact, this promise of the coming of Christ, Paul at one point describes as a "secret wisdom" of God, which God decreed (προορίζω — pro'oridzo, predestined) before the ages. 1 Corinthians 2:7.

[132] It should be noted in discussing Omnipotence that the doctrine of God's omnipotence does not mean that he can do anything. God cannot lie, he cannot sin, he cannot cease to be God, he cannot alter his character, etc... These are not limitations on God, these are simply realities created by a God who is not irrational. Thus, omnipotence is correctly defined as God's ability to do anything that is consistent with his character and his will.

[133] τῇ ὡρισμένῃ βουλῇ (te horismene boule) — a plan that has been previously set in place and now brought to completion.

[134] Noting too that Peter is clearly stating that while the decree of God was that Jesus be crucified for the sins of the elect, the means by which God chose to accomplish it was by the hands of wicked men — certainly even their wills conformed to the plan of God.

[135] Acts 13:48. Note that it is those who are decreed to eternal life that believe,

The Timetable of the Decree

Though it has been implied above, for clarity it is valuable for us to raise the question as to when God decrees who he will elect. This brings us back to Paul's letter to the Ephesians where he speaks of the election taking place "before the foundations of the earth." Often, when we speak of the elect as a group of names, we speak of the Lamb's Book of Life.[136] In Revelation, we even find this idea being described in the negative, for those whose names are not in the Lamb's Book of Life are cast into the fires of hell.[137] Furthermore, Jesus speaks of the kingdom of God as that which has been prepared for the elect since the foundation of the world[138], reminding us again that it was God's design (decree) from eternity that after making the world perfect, mankind would fall into sin and that he would send his Son to take on flesh and to intercede for the sins of his elect.

Single or Double Election?

Some object to the question of election based on the belief that if God elects some to heaven and if he elects others to damnation, that makes God the author of sin. The logic of the argument flows in this fashion. If it is God who elects before the foundation of the world and he elects some to destruction, he must also elect that they

---

not those who believe who are decreed to have eternal life. The decree of God precedes the belief.

[136] Philippians 4:3; Revelation 3:5, 21:27.

[137] Revelation 13:8, 17:8.

[138] Matthew 25:34. Matthew also alludes to this same idea (Matthew 13:35) in the explanation as to the nature of Jesus' teaching, quoting not only Psalm 78:2 but also alluding to Isaiah 42:9 and Amos 3:7, pointing out that his coming and teaching is the revealing of those things hidden from the beginning of time — were God not to have ordained these things from the beginning, there would have been no content to what Jesus and the prophets referred to as mystery.

sin in a way that would earn them destruction and thus is the one ultimately responsible for their sin. This objection has led to a debate as to how God handles or elects the reprobate. Does he actively elect them to hell even before they did anything good or evil or does he passively allow them to follow into judgment based on their own actions and inherited guilt?

Within Reformed circles, people fall into two categories in this debate — that of those holding to "single-election" and that of those holding to "double-election."[139] The single view holds that God elects some to salvation in an active sense and then chooses to pass over those he will not save. The double view holds that just as God elects some to salvation, he elects others to damnation.

The majority of the Reformed Confessions have chosen to articulate a "single-election" point of view when it comes to this matter, adopting language of God permitting some to face the just punishment for their sins and others to be elected to glory. Similarly, the majority of Reformed theologians today seem to fall into that camp. A smaller group within the Reformed witness would follow Calvin's lead and embrace the idea of God's actively electing some to glory and actively electing others to damnation, as being more faithful to the description given by the Apostle Paul in Romans 9:19-22.[140]

DOES ALL OF THIS MAKE A DIFFERENCE?

How then does an understanding of these views affect one's thought? First, if God's election is unconditional — namely, if we can do nothing to earn it or merit it in any way — then it ought to

---

[139] The position one holds here roughly corresponds to one's view on the Lapsarian argument, discussed briefly in the chapter on the Ordo Salutus.

[140] A view that this author would also support.

foster in our hearts a profound sense of humility. Paul writes that salvation is by God's grace for the express purpose that it leaves no room for the boasting of men.[141] It is God's doing, not ours, so we can only boast in Christ.[142]

Secondly, this forces us to adopt a theocentric rather than an anthrocentric system of theology. In other words, all that we understand in our theology and religion needs to revolve around God and not men. How quickly we are prone to lose sight of that important truth, yet it is God's free grace in which we find our hope and life and the teaching and preaching of his grace stymies all of our attempts to honor ourselves.

---

[141] Ephesians 2:9.

[142] Galatians 6:14.

Chapter 11
Limited Atonement

Of all five points of the Tulip, in my experience teaching this material, this is by far the doctrine that brings the most resistance. Because of this resistance, theologians in various circles have sometimes adopted different names for this doctrine, like "Definite Atonement" and "Particular Redemption," but regardless of the name given to the doctrine, the content remains the same.

The question that is ultimately asked is, "For whom did Christ die in a saving sense?" Calvinists and Neo-Arminians largely agree that even unbelievers benefit from the sacrifice of Christ through God's Common Grace — rain is given to the just and to the unjust alike.[143] The bottom line is that were God to never have ordained that his Son would come and redeem the elect, God would have entered into final judgment in the Garden when Adam and Eve sinned. None of us would even have had the benefit of the common joys of life, like friendships, love, good food, and the joy of seeing children smile and laugh as they play. These are good gifts that both the believer and the unbeliever enjoys, but these are gifts that belong to this earthly sphere and will pass away in death.

What is of importance here is the question of who benefits

---
[143] Matthew 5:45.

from the death of Christ in an eternal sense? The Neo-Arminian would say that Jesus died to save all mankind, but that it is up to us whether we accept or reject the benefits that He offers. In contrast, the Calvinist argues that Jesus did not die for all of mankind, but only for those whom God elected. Calvinists sometimes paraphrase their view by saying that while Jesus' atoning sacrifice is sufficient for all, it is only efficient for the elect.[144]

Owen's Logic

John Owen[145] provided one of the best logical defenses of this doctrine that has been produced, found in his writings against Arminianism. Owen pointed out that if one logically asked the question, "for what sins did Christ die?", there are only four real answers that could possibly be given to the question and only one that makes logical or Biblical sense.[146]

- *Answer 1 — Christ died for none of the sins of all of the*

---

[144] This is one reason that some Calvinists are uncomfortable with the term "limited" in connection with the atonement. They want to be clear that the reason that Jesus died only for the elect was not that the effect of his atonement was limited in power, that he could only save so many and the rest were lost. Instead, the power of the atonement is great and mighty enough to save any and all; the limitation that is placed upon it is not of power, but of degree, for God's decree is that the elect would be saved and those not elected would face the just punishment for their sins.

[145] John Owen (1616-1683) was an English Non-Conformist, the Chaplain for Oliver Cromwell, and instructor at Oxford University and one of the finest thinkers of his day. He is also responsible for underwriting the publication of John Bunyan's classic, *Pilgrim's Progress*. Owen's seven-volume commentary on the Book of Hebrews still stands today as one of the great authoritative works on the text.

[146] With this approach, Owen is applying categories of logical argumentation that are still foundational in formal logic today.

people. Of course, this answer we must dismiss outright, for it makes Christ's work entirely ineffectual and makes the idea of salvation reliant entirely upon the works of an individual. Such was ultimately the position of Pelagius, whom we mentioned earlier in this book. Given, too, our sinful state, all mankind becomes lost and the devil effectively is seen as frustrating Jesus' work. It is a position that leads quickly away from the scriptural testimony and into both heresy and utter despair, for no hope can be found when we rely on our own works or on the works of a fallen church to save us.

- *Answer 2 — Christ died for some of the sins of all of the people.* Like the above answer, this makes no sense. All sin must be atoned for if a man is to enter into God's presence and as sinners, all our works are dung in God's economy.[147]
- *Answer 3 — Christ died for all of the sins of all of the people.* This view is universalism. The problem with this view is that Scripture does not support it. In fact, Jesus speaks more about the reality of Hell than any other Biblical person and when Jesus speaks of Hell's reality, he also speaks of Hell being populated. Were the atonement universal, then Hell would be devoid of population apart from the fallen angels. Such a view also makes nonsense of the absolute statements that Jesus makes, like that of "no man comes to the Father except through Me."[148]
- *Answer 4 — Christ died for all of the sins of some of the people.* This is the view of Calvinism's Limited Atonement. Jesus' work on the cross is 100% effectual for those whom God has elected to be brought to himself. Jesus said, "No one comes to me unless the Father first draws him and I will

---

[147] Philippians 3:8.

[148] John 14:6.

raise him up on the last day."[149]

The Wesleyan/Neo-Arminian would accept answer three with one nuance. He would argue that while Christ died for all the sins of all the people, it is up to the person to believe and accept that gift of grace. Owen responded to this nuance by posing the question as to whether unbelief is a sin. If unbelief is not a sin, how can they be judged for their unbelief? If unbelief is a sin, then it has been atoned for (under this model) and again, how can that person be judged. If it is a sin and is not atoned for, then we are reduced to answer 2 and everything is lost. Owen further pointed out that Jesus was clear that unbelief is a sin that condemns people to Hell.[150] A further problem with this Neo-Arminian view is that if people have the ultimate decision as to whether the atoning work of Christ is applied to them, it leaves open the possibility that no one would be saved, thus making Christ's work on the cross totally ineffectual, again a view that is not only contrary to scripture but contrary to the character of God to allow such a universal failure to take place.

THE STATE OF BEING AT-ONE

We have spoken a great deal about Christ's atoning work for us, but as of yet, we have not offered a basic definition for the term. On the most basic level, the work of atonement is a work that reestablishes a relationship that has been severed — it restores two parties to a relationship in which they can be spoken of as "at-one." A synonym for atonement is reconciliation. While there is a great deal we could say about the specific atoning work of Christ, what is most important for us in this context is the principle that when

---

[149] John 6:44.

[150] John 8:23-24.

atonement is being worked, specific parties are always in view. Generic, unknown masses do not atone with each other; instead a specific person is atoned with another specific person — there is always a personal nature.

And if there is a personal nature, then those persons must have been known by God from eternity and certainly by Christ on the cross. Yet, such knowledge is impossible unless the atoning work is for a definite or a limited group of people — in Biblical terms, for the elect — those whose names have been written in the Lamb's Book of Life from before the foundation of the earth.

The Neo-Arminian would counter that while the work of atonement is real and personal, the atonement is always a potential atonement (universally applied) and becomes definite only when accepted by the individual person. Yet when we see atonement spoken of in the Bible, it is never spoken of as a potential atonement, but always an actual one. For example, on the Old Testament Day of Atonement[151], the sacrifices offered by the priests were understood to bring actual atonement for the people of Israel — a numerous, but definite group of people. The propitiatory work of the priest was always considered effective.[152]

Even when applied on an individual level, the work of atonement was not considered potential. For example, God set forth that if a person sins against one of their fellow Israelites, confession of the sin should be accompanied by a payment of restitution[153] and a ram sacrificed to work atonement.[154] This was said to bring atonement between God and the sinner as well as between the sinner and the person he offended — in fact, the one offended did not have

---

[151] Leviticus 16 goes into detail to explain the Day of Atonement.

[152] Propitiation is defined as the work that brings atonement and in the New Testament, Jesus is spoken of as our propitiation (1 John 2:2).

[153] In this case, the damage done, plus 20%.

[154] Numbers 5:5-10.

recourse to come back and sue for a higher restitution payment. God considered the matter over with and expected people to follow suit in their interactions with each other. The atonement was actual as well as definite.

A Shepherd and His Sheep

The Bible regularly provides examples of the definite nature of the atonement, but there is probably none so poignant as that of the Good Shepherd dying for his sheep. In the Old Testament, God speaks of the many leaders he has sent to shepherd his people[155] though in most cases they do a very poor job, putting their own needs ahead of those whom they are called to serve.[156] God promises the people that he himself will come to shepherd the people[157], seeking the lost, binding the injured, and strengthening the weak. He connects this prophesy with that of Micah[158] when he also says that as he shepherds the people himself, it will be in the person of his servant, David.[159]

Jesus, then connects this Messianic prophesy to himself when he calls himself "the Good Shepherd."[160] In the context of this passage, Jesus makes some important statements about his sheep, namely that he lays his life down for his sheep.[161] Jesus is clear that

---

[155] 2 Samuel 7:7.

[156] See God's condemnation of the "hired hands" in Ezekiel 34:2-10. Similar language is also found in 2 Peter 2 and Jude of false pastors who prey on churches to suit their own ends.

[157] Ezekiel 34:15.

[158] Micah 5:4.

[159] Ezekiel 34:25. A return of a Davidic King was one of the more significant aspects of the Messianic promises — see 2 Samuel 7:12-16.

[160] John 10:14.

[161] John 10:11.

he does not lay his life down for all sheep without distinction, but only for his sheep. So, who are Jesus' sheep? Jesus answers that question in the same passage. Jesus' sheep are those who hear the voice of Christ[162] and follow him.[163] Jesus clearly states that the Jews that were persecuting him were not of his flock[164] and it is only to his flock that he gives eternal life with the iron-clad promise that no one will snatch them out of his hands.[165]

We find similar language in other parts of the Bible as well. For example, in what we refer to as Jesus' "High Priestly Prayer," he speaks of those whom God has given him from the world repeatedly.[166] In fact, he goes as far as to say that he *is not* praying for the world without exception, but specifically for those who the Father has given him[167] and for those who will come to faith through their word.[168] Peter clearly articulates this idea as well when he states that God is capable of both "keeping the unrighteous under judgment while preserving the godly."[169] Likewise, Paul will state, "who can bring any charge against God's elect — for God is the one who justifies them!"[170]

---

[162] This is what we refer to as the "Effectual Call,"discussed further under the chapter on the Ordo Salutus.

[163] John 10:27.

[164] John 10:26. This implies clearly that Jesus knows not only his own but also those who are not his own in a definite way.

[165] John 10:28. Note that this also speaks to the doctrine of the Perseverance of the Saints.

[166] John 17:2,9,12,24.

[167] John 17:9.

[168] John 17:20.

[169] 2 Peter 2:9. Note, if God does not know who those are in a definite way, how can he be said to do this?

[170] Romans 8:33.

OBJECTIONS: ANY AND ALL PASSAGES

There are several passages of scripture that are often brought up by those wanting to support Neo-Arminianism in opposition to the doctrine of Limited Atonement. These passages, taken alone, seem to imply a love that God has for all of mankind and a desire that he has that all men come to faith and not any should perish.

Before we look at these passages in context, we should address what is typically called the "reformational principle of Biblical interpretation." This principle is built on the recognition that Scripture is the inerrant word of God and thus is able to interpret itself. Two rules of interpretation then come out of this principle: first, that what may appear on the surface to be a contradiction really is not one and second, that where there is a vague or questionable teaching, the clear texts are used to interpret the unclear texts and the clear majority of witnesses is used to interpret the minority texts. Thus, if there are ten texts that speak of a particular doctrine and only two that seem in opposition to the ten, then the two need to be understood in light of the ten.

FOR GOD SO LOVED THE WORLD...

Probably the most common objection to Limited Atonement that I hear is that of a misunderstanding of John 3:16. People in America are brought up memorizing the text and assuming that it is a statement of God's universal love for mankind, or more specifically, that Jesus died for all of mankind without exception.

To begin with, we need to recognize the context of the verse, in particular interpreting it in light of the verses that surround it. For example, John goes on to say in verse 18 that those who do not believe are "already condemned." If faith and salvation are openly offered to all and reliant on a person's will to believe in the Gospel, then how can they be "already condemned"? The only way that such could be the case is were God to have elected some to glory and others to judgment, some to come to his Son in faith and others to reject Christ in disbelief.

Secondly, we should note the little English word, "so." In Greek, this is the word οὕτως (houtos). Literally, it means, "in this way." The problem is that in modern English, most people read this word as meaning "so much." Yet, in English in the 1600s, the word "so" referred not so much to quantity but, like the Greek, to a way in which something was to be done — it was to be done "just so." Yet, as English has changed, our translations have not. Nevertheless, what the passage, correctly understood, is saying is that "God loved the world in this way, that he gave his only begotten Son…" The sending of Jesus becomes the demonstration of God's love, not the result of God's love. When you understand the text in this way it entirely changes how even the broader passage is understood. For what is taught is that God demonstrates his love for the world[171] by the redeeming of believers from judgment through the sacrifice of his Son and the condemnation of those who will reject him, for they are receiving their just desserts for their wickedness.

ONCE AND FOR ALL …

For some, Hebrews 10:10 also poses a challenge to the doctrine of Limited Atonement. Does this not say that Jesus died once and for all? Indeed it does, but not the way that most understand the text. The word used here, which is translated as "all," is the

---

[171] The word "world" here is the Greek word, κόσμος (cosmos), which is variously used in the scriptures to refer to all of the created order, outer space, just earth, or mankind — context becomes the key to understanding the term.

Greek word, ἐφάπαξ (ephapax), which speaks of excluding further occurrences. In other words, the "once and for all" is not saying that Jesus' sacrifice is done once and for all people, but instead is saying that Jesus' sacrifice is made once and for all time — never to be repeated.

DESIRES ALL PEOPLE TO BE SAVED ...

Does God really desire that every person without exception be saved? Do the damnation of the unbelievers represent Satan's frustrations to God's designs? Certainly such ought not be said of our God. The passage in question comes from 1 Timothy 2:4, a passage, when taken out of context, sounds an awful lot like God wants everybody to be saved. Yet, in the context of the passage, Paul is instructing Timothy to pray for all kinds of people (including kings, leaders, etc...). Thus, in context, what is being said is that God's design and desires are that people from every different walk of life and vocation come into the body of Christ. Thus, it is not saying that God wants everyone without exception to be saved, but everyone without distinction of race or social class.[172]

FOR THE SINS OF THE WHOLE WORLD ...

As John presents his case for the atonement, he refers to Jesus as the propitiation for our sins.[173] Again, context is the key to understanding this statement. At the end of chapter 1, John is writing about seeking forgiveness by confessing our sins (the act of a

---

[172] Galatians 3:28.

[173] 1 John 2:2.

believer) and that in Christ we have an advocate — a paraclete[174] — in Christ Jesus. Here, it is clear that John is speaking to believers — the elect — and thus the statement that follows should be understood in the same way. Thus, Jesus is not the propitiation for the whole world without any exceptions[175], but for the elect that come from all of the nations of the world.

NOT WISHING THAT ANY SHOULD PERISH ...

2 Peter 3:9 again raises a question in the eyes of many Neo-Arminians. They say, "Look, God doesn't want anyone in the world to perish, but obviously some do, so clearly God is leaving the decision up to us — His desire would be that all people are saved." But as we look at the larger context once again, we find the Apostle Peter writing something very different. Specifically he has been discussing God's judgment upon the wicked[176] and then the charge that the wicked raise that everything has remained the same — where is the return of your Christ?[177]

Peter answers this challenge by pointing out that God is demonstrating his patience.[178] Why? Because he does not desire that any (of his elect) would perish. This is the only possible reading

---

[174] A Paraclete was an advocate with the court on your behalf who is doing so not for payment nor as an officer of the court, but as one who has standing with the judge and has a vested interest in you individually and personally. The Paraclete secures the release of the person on trial not because of the person's merits, but because of the merits of the Paraclete in the eyes of the judge (note again the personal nature of this action — it cannot be personal if Jesus does not know for whom he is dying).

[175] Then we would have universalism, for as God, Jesus' sacrifice must be seen as being effective.

[176] 2 Peter 2.

[177] 2 Peter 3:1-7.

[178] 2 Peter 3:8-9.

of the text, because if one reads it otherwise, then God is unable to fulfill his promise of eternal life if we reject it, making the human will greater than the will of God.

While one might sight a few other passages that speak along these lines, these passages are comparatively few when lined up with the repeated references to a sovereign God choosing to call his own to himself and guaranteeing those who believe eternal life. Without a sovereign God, then we can have no guarantees and all lies on our ability to live out what God commands of us — a dangerous view given our tendency toward sin. Furthermore, when understood in context, these passages do not necessarily teach a Neo-Arminian view on salvation.

Evangelism

A final criticism that is not exegetical, but practical, is often raised. And that is, if God has elected people to himself anyway, then why bother evangelizing? The answer to that question is hopefully obvious. First, God has commanded us to do so — he gives us the privilege of participating in his redemptive work. Second, because we do not know the list of names found in the Lamb's Book of Life, thus, we don't know who God is and is not calling to himself, so we are motivated to make him known to all.[179]

Remember, in this light, it is important to note that even those who are not elect do benefit from the sacrifice of Jesus. Apart from

---

[179] 2 Corinthians 2:14; 5:20. Historically, it has been Calvinists who have led the modern Missionary movement — Calvin himself sent missionaries not only throughout Europe, but as far away as Brazil. Not evangelizing would lead us into the heresy of "hyper-Calvinism."

Common Grace, unbelievers have benefitted from the changed lives lived by believers. Christians not only founded the first hospitals but have founded more hospitals than any other organization. Christians have been the first to put their lives and health at risk to minister to those with the Plague, with Leprosy, and with other horrendous diseases. Though many Christians justified their slavery, it was Christians who put an end to the British and American forms of slavery and it is Christians who are still actively at work seeking to bring slavery to an end in other parts of the globe — especially of that most heinous kind of sex-slave-trade that is still rampant in the world. Christians have stood against injustice, have ministered to the poor and hurting, have created schools and educational systems, and given written languages and dictionaries to many of the world's cultures. We do all of this for one reason — to earn the right to share the best news of all with any the Lord will lead in our direction. In this context, even the hardened atheist benefits, for the entire society is lifted up.

How do We Evangelize?

A question is raised in the context of evangelism that is worth noting. The question is, can we tell people that God loves them? Surely, we do not know whether they are elect or not, so, is this approach to evangelism appropriate?

While many people have been taught that the way to begin an evangelistic discussion is through a phrase like, "God loves you," that model is not found in the Bible. The Biblical model is "Repent and believe,"[180] which carries entirely different connotations. When Paul went into a new city, he first reasoned with the Jews in the

---

[180] Mark 1:15; Luke 24:47; Acts 2:37-39; 20:21.

synagogue from the scriptures[181] and then, when rejected by the Jews, would reason with the gentiles of the city wherever he was given the opportunity. Again, we never find him offering a blanket statement that "Jesus loves you."

Does Jesus love those to whom we evangelize? If they are believers, the answer is clearly, "yes." If they are unbelievers, the answer is clearly, "yes, but in a common-grace kind of way." If you are asking about love in a saving kind of way, the answer is, "we don't know — maybe." Should that uncertainty stymie our evangelistic efforts? Not at all, that is if we approach evangelism in a Biblical way. So preach and preach boldly. Invite people to repent and profess faith in Jesus Christ and live. Yet know that it is the Lord of the Harvest who gives life to the souls of dead sinners and he will draw whom he has chosen.

---

[181] Acts 17:17; 18:4; 18:19; 19:8.

CHAPTER 12
IRRESISTIBLE GRACE[182]

The question that we who are Reformed regularly raise with the Neo-Arminians is "Can God's plans be frustrated by the actions of the Devil?" Our answer is, "no; God is sovereign." Even the wickedness that the Devil plans and does is done with the permission of God and brings about the end which our Lord has designed. Thus, when we talk of the grace of God, we recognize that it is not resistible in an ultimate sense. Certainly many of us can testify to having sought to resist God's grace for a season, but like a great fisherman, God was simply giving us a little more line and wearing out our resistance with the hook still firmly lodged in our lip. We may fight his call, but the timing of our being "reeled in" is entirely in God's hands.

THE FORCEFUL WOOING OF GOD

God calls us with his grace, drawing us to himself through his Son, Jesus Christ. But how strong or effective is that calling? The

---

[182] In the sense that Grace and Calling coincide (see later section on the Ordo Salutus), this doctrine is sometimes referred to as that of "Effectual Calling."

Prophet Hosea provides for us a very clear picture of God drawing his people to himself. Hosea writes:

"With ropes of leather and cords of love, I pulled them. I was with them as one who lifts a yoke onto them and I reached out to them and fed them."

(Hosea 11:4)

In context, this is the "Out of Egypt I called my Son" passage and God is describing the calling of his people out of their slavery, something that will be fulfilled in a spiritual way with the work of his Son, Jesus, as we are called away from our slavery to sin. He begins with a contrast — ropes of leather and cords of love. The calling of God, as one preacher said, is done with a carrot and a 2x4. God draws us graciously with his love, but when we are stubborn (as pack animals commonly are), he does not stop drawing us, he just changes to a more forceful method.

The Hebrew term for "draw" that is employed here is מָשַׁךְ (mashak), which means "to draw along." It is the term that would be used to describe the pulling along of a stubborn beast in the direction his master wished it to go. That coupled with the idea of the yoke[183] — a restraining device designed to lead an animal in the direction the master wishes it to go — paints for us a rather unflattering portrait of ourselves in the hands of God. It portrays our stubborn resistance, but God overcoming that resistance with the tools of his trade.

As unflattering as this language may sound, it is language picked up in the New Testament as well. Jesus stated that no one can come to the Father unless the Father first draws him to Christ.[184]

---

[183] Note that as believers, while given freedom in Christ, that does not mean we live as wild beasts, permitted to anything. True freedom only comes when we are in the greatest submission to Christ Jesus and the picture of the yoke is meant to be a reminder to us of that great truth. The ancient Mishnas speak of taking the yoke of the Law upon your neck — Jesus instead said to take his yoke, for his was light (Matthew 11:29-30).

[184] John 6:44.

The word that Jesus employs here is the Greek word, ειλκω (elko), which refers to one pulling an object from one point to another. This term is used to describe the way a fisherman hauls a loaded net onto his boat[185] or the way one might be forcefully drug out of a place.[186] Thus, the picture we find here is of God forcefully drawing out of all mankind a group of people to hand to the Son without the possibility of his failure or of them falling away.[187]

THE WHOM OF THE DRAWING

This ought to be one of those obvious questions, but for the sake of the discussion, it is perhaps useful to reinforce that we do not have any part in the drawing of ourselves. God does so. We have already mentioned Jesus' statement about the Father's drawing of the elect to the Son[188]; in addition, Jesus speaks of drawing[189] all men to himself.[190] Paul echoes this language in his writings, stating that we have been reconciled to God through the death and life of the Son.[191] In addition, it is God who saves us, not by our own works, but by his holy calling and mercy.[192] Even as Ezekiel promises the fulfillment of the covenant in the Messiah, he similarly records God

---

[185] John 21:6,11.

[186] Acts 16:19; 21:30.

[187] Also see John 10:26-30 of God drawing people out in such a way that they will not fall away.

[188] John 6:44.

[189] Same word, ἕλκω.

[190] John 12:32. We did not speak of this passage specifically in the last chapter, but again, in context, Jesus is speaking of all the elect coming from all the nations of the world, for he is speaking of people becoming the children of light.

[191] Romans 5:10 — notice the passive use of the verbs.

[192] 2 Timothy 1:9; Titus 3:5.

saying: "I will cause you to walk in my statutes."[193]

GOD WINS

The end of this doctrine is the simple truth that God wins. This is not an accident, it is worked by His design and it was determined from before the foundation of the earth. When God sets himself to work toward an end, there is nothing on earth or in heaven that can stop him from that end. And that is good news, because it means that the promise is to keep us and preserve us in his hand through this life and into his presence[194] is sure. And we can rely on that.

---

[193] Ezekiel 36:27.
[194] John 10:28.

CHAPTER 13
THE PERSEVERANCE OF THE SAINTS

In many ways, this doctrine is the logical conclusion to the four points that have preceded it. If God does the saving and if God is the one working in us, then God will complete the work he started in us. Such is the Apostle Paul's language of the Golden chain in Romans 8:28-30. Believers are described as being "united with Christ"[195] and those with whom he is united, he will not let go.[196] This does not mean that once a believer is brought to Christ, they can sit back and live however they want to live with a free pass to glory; may we never think that way.[197] What the doctrine is saying is that because God has done this work in us we have become different people — new men and women — and thus our desire should not be to return to our wicked ways, but to live out of a sense of gratitude toward God and thus we will persevere in faith until our dying days.[198]

---

[195] Romans 6:5-14; 1 John 1:3.

[196] John 6:37.

[197] Romans 6:1-2.

[198] This is also in recognition that it is only because of the power of the Holy Spirit working within us that we can persevere in faith. Note too, that this is not a doctrine that a Wesleyan can consistently hold to for if salvation rests in our

Misnomers

Sometimes this doctrine is worded in ways that are unhelpful to those seeking to live out the doctrine. In certain circles the language of "Once Saved — Always Saved," is used, yet this language can lead people to see the Christian life as passive and neglect working out our salvation with fear and trembling[199], seeking to actively live a life to honor God. While our justification[200] is worked out once and for all time before God, our sanctification is ongoing and progressive until we reach glory. The Bible never teaches that if we pray a certain prayer or go to the altar once that all will be eternally fine with our souls. Instead, the Bible teaches that believers do confess their sins and profess faith, but the change that is worked by God within them is a life-long change.

In other circles, this doctrine is referred to as "Eternal Preservation." While this language does do a better job of reflecting God's activity in preserving a people for himself[201], it still does not reflect the idea that we are also called to participate in our own sanctification, not to lay back and passively enjoy the ride. Thus, "Perseverance" is the term that is typically chosen within Reformed circles as it reflects the labor of the Christian to put sin to death in their life all the while recognizing that the power to do so comes from God alone.

---

choice to follow Christ, then we can potentially lose it and die separated from Christ.

[199] Philippians 2:12.

[200] For more on justification, see the chapter on the Ordo Salutus.

[201] See 1 Kings 19:18. In Hebrew, the phrase is, "I have preserved for myself" — the verbal language is causative. Paul picks up on this in Romans 11:4 when he cites this passage.

The Logical Conclusion

As mentioned, this doctrine is the logical conclusion of the doctrines of the Tulip that precede it. We have already discussed Perkins' Golden Chain[202] noting the significance of the linguistic connections of each link of that chain and the confidence of the Apostle Paul that the good work that God begins in a believer will be brought to completion.[203] Again, with God in the driver's seat, his will and designs are accomplished and he will preserve his own until they arrive at glory. Similarly, the Apostle Paul speaks of being guarded through faith for a salvation that has already been prepared for him.[204] And, of course, note the certainty with which Jesus makes this statement about believers: He says, "Amen, Amen, I say to you that the one who hears my word and believes the one who sent me, he has eternal life and into judgment he will not go, instead, he will pass from death into life."[205] In these comments, there is no conditional language, but instead it presents a promise to the believer that if you genuinely come to faith in Jesus Christ, you will not lose that faith but will remain a believer into glory.

Objections: Turning Back to Your Vomit...

Like with our discussion of Limited Atonement, there are some passages of scripture that, if taken out of context, can be made to sound as if they teach you can lose your salvation — one of which is found in Peter's second letter where he speaks of a believer who

---

[202] Romans 8:29-30.

[203] Philippians 1:6.

[204] 1 Peter 1:5.

[205] John 5:24.

falls back into sin being like a dog returning to its vomit.[206] Yet, in this case, it is speaking of the mess that comes into the life of a person who, after coming to faith, backslides — not who loses his salvation. Genuine believers, while not losing salvation, are capable of backsliding in their faith for many different reasons. The difference is that one who is a genuine believer will repent from their sliding and return to walking in faith.

THOSE ONCE ENLIGHTENED...

The most common objection, when speaking of the idea of a believer falling away, is found in Hebrews 6:4-8. This passage, the Wesleyan would argue, proves that it is possible for a genuine believer to fall from the faith and never be returned to faith in Christ, yet, when one looks closely, the text speaks of something different.

To begin with, there is nothing within the text that necessarily demands that the people in question were genuine believers, only that they were members of the visible church[207] and enjoying its blessings. If we look at the passage more closely, we will find out that these people who fall away have experienced the church in four ways:
1. They are described as being "once enlightened."[208] This suggests some understanding of the Gospel at least on an

---

[206] 2 Peter 2:20-22.

[207] Theologians typically distinguish between the visible and the invisible church: The visible church being made up of everyone that might attend a worship service or be active in the life of the institutional church in the world, the invisible church being made up of all genuine believers in Jesus Christ. Thus, all of the invisible church is part of the visible church, but not all of the visible church is part of the invisible church.

[208] The verb φωτίζω (photidzo) is used here, which means to shine light upon or to illuminate something.

intellectual level, but not necessarily on a spiritual level. The term refers to an exposure to the truth, not necessarily accepting it. Many in the scriptures sat under the teaching of the Gospel but never accepted it for themselves.[209]

2. They are described as having "tasted the heavenly gift."[210] While often this is used to describe one's eating of food, its literal meaning refers to the act of taste and can also refer to the way one might taste-test small samples of food at a sampling. Note, then, the emphasis here is on one's outward experience, not on inward relationship. Jesus said that it is not what goes into the mouth that defiles, but what comes out of it[211]; the same can be said to be true in the opposite — it is not what goes into our mouth that purifies, but the profession of faith that comes from a change worked by the Spirit within.

3. They are described as "sharing in the Holy Spirit."[212] On the outset, this may seem the more challenging to explain because we typically think of the Holy Spirit in terms of His indwelling within us as believers. Yet, the term really refers to being in the presence of the Holy Spirit, not necessarily having him indwell; and those being spoken of have had just that experience as they have fellowshipped with genuine believers who have been indwelt by the Spirit. Interestingly, the author of Hebrews uses this term more often than any other author. While he uses the term several ways, when applying the term to humans, he seems to use it to refer to the

---

[209] Judas Iscariot is a prime example here.

[210] The verb here is γεύομαι (geuomai), which refers to tasting food, not necessarily consuming the whole meal.

[211] Matthew 15:11.

[212] The verb here is μέτοχος (metochos), meaning to share time or companionship with another.

visible church, not to the invisible church. His qualification is that one demonstrates that they have genuinely shared in Christ if they persevere in faith until the end.[213]

4. They have "tasted the goodness of the Word." Notice that this is a repeat of the same language used above of "tasting the heavenly gift." The reality is that many have been given a taste of the Word of God, through preaching, evangelism, reading, friends, family, etc... yet have walked away still eternally blind. Many of the blind will only ever see the earthly wisdom and benefits and never be captured by the eternal wisdom and benefits. Why? Because the Holy Spirit has not begun a work in them.

WARNINGS AGAINST FALLING...

A group of texts that is often brought up in opposition to the doctrine of the Perseverance of the Saints are those texts that contain warnings against falling away.[214] The logic behind this argument is that if it were not possible for a genuine believer to fall away then why bother with issuing a warning? The question can be approached in two ways. First, given that the Biblical Epistles were written to the visible church and not just to the church invisible, such warnings were pronounced to warn those without saving faith of the consequences of falling away and to prick their souls to repent and come to Christ — something made effectual by the Holy Spirit. The second way to approach the question is to recognize that warning signs are always posted in our society to warn people of

---

[213] Hebrews 3:14 — sounds a lot like the doctrine of the Perseverance of the Saints...

[214] Such as: 1 Corinthians 10:11-12; Colossians 1:22-23; Romans 11:20-21; and Revelation 2:5 (notice, too, that the passages in Romans and Revelation speak of groups of people, not individuals).

this or that behavior. It is expected that people heed those signs, but to remove temptation, the signs are posted in public. Such could be a scriptural equivalent to the warning sign near a sharp bend in the road or around a swimming pool.

"I NEVER KNEW YOU..."

This passage in the sermon on the mount[215] is also cited against the doctrine of the Persecution of the Saints. In such an objection it will be pointed out that those being rejected by Jesus are crying out, "Lord, Lord!" and thus thought of themselves as believers. Nevertheless, they are cast away. To answer this, we must recognize that the Hebraic idea of knowledge speaks of a relationship and thus, the "I never knew you" is taken to mean, "I never knew you relationally" or "I was never in a relationship with you personally and individually." Clearly these people are not genuine believers and have never been so, for they are described as "workers of lawlessness," but given their mindset, it seems that they were members of a church — just for all of the wrong reasons. Thus, this is not a falling away from salvation, only a falling away from the church.

HYMENAEUS AND ALEXANDER[216]

Sometimes it is suggested that these men once had faith and then fell away. Yet the language we see here is that Paul is handing

---

[215] Matthew 7:21-23.

[216] 1 Timothy 1:20 — note that Hymenaeus is mentioned again in 2 Timothy 2:17 along with a Philetus and Alexander is quite possibly the same Alexander who was the coppersmith mentioned in 2 Timothy 4:14 who had done Paul harm.

these men over "to Satan" for a season in the hopes that they will repent. In fact, each time this phrase is used[217], it is used in the context of church discipline, not in the context of someone eternally falling away.[218]

SCATTERING THE SEED...

Jesus' parable of the sower scattering the seed[219] provides us with an excellent description of how evangelism works and how the genuine believer in Jesus Christ will persevere in faith until the end (thus bearing good fruit). The parable is simple, there is a sower scattering seed indiscriminately (just as we preach the Gospel to all people who will listen). As the sower scatters, the seed falls on various types of soil.

As we would expect, the good soil represents the believer and when the seed falls in his or her life, it grows, blossoms, and bears good fruit. But Jesus does not stop with speaking of the seed falling on good soil. It falls on other types of soil as well. That which falls on the road is trampled underfoot and never takes root. That which falls on rocky soil develops no root system and thus falls away when tribulation comes. And that which falls on thorny soil is choked out by cares and earthly riches.

While the good soil and the hardened soil of the road is pretty obvious as to people-types, what of the lives in whom the

---

[217] 1 Corinthians 5:5; 1 Timothy 1:20. Notice too, Paul's hope that those in question will repent and return to the church fellowship.

[218] Note that some would take this language as Paul's application of "the Keys of the Kingdom" (see Matthew 16:19), yet the context of Jesus' statement recorded by Matthew seems to be that of evangelism, not discipline. Furthermore, salvation is clearly presented as being about an individual's relationship to Jesus Christ mediated by no one (1 Timothy 2:5).

[219] Mark 4:1-20.

seed begins to grow but does not grow mature. Is this genuine faith for a season? Before we answer that question, though, we need to answer the question as to what makes the difference between the rocky/thorny soil and the good soil? The answer, of course, is that good soil is prepared ahead of time — that is what makes it good. It has been tilled, fertilized, and irrigated, not to mention having straight rows hoed into it. Then and only then will it take the seed and allow the seed to grow healthy, strong, and in a way that bears fruit. Obviously, in the analogy, the Holy Spirit is the one who prepares the soil — which means he has not prepared the soil marked by rocks or thorns. Lest one is born again they will never see the kingdom[220] — thus the "faith" found in the rocks and thorns is not so much a saving faith worked by the Holy Spirit, but an emotional or an intellectual faith worked by the events of someone's situation, but never being transformative. As a result, we live in a culture where many atheists spent their formative years in church. Until the Spirit prepares the soil, the seed of the Gospel cannot grow. Many will live their lives in connection with the church[221], but the true believer will bear fruit in keeping with repentance.[222]

Assurance

As humans, one of the things that we long for is assurance. We long for the assurance that we are loved by our spouses and by our friends. We long for the assurance that there is a way out of the mess in which we happen to find ourselves. We long to know that

---

[220] John 3:3.

[221] Jesus tells a parable about the Kingdom of God growing like a seed, though small, becoming a great tree under which the birds of the air will find a place to nest. This passage is an allusion to Ezekiel 17:22-24, but presents to us a reminder that the Church (the tree) will find grateful unbelievers in its midst (the birds).

[222] Matthew 3:8; Galatians 5:22-24.

the God we serve will follow through on fulfilling his promises in this life and in the next. This assurance gives us confidence and it gives us hope.

The Doctrine of the Perseverance of the Saints is the ultimate scriptural confirmation of this assurance — it is the logical and scriptural end to the Golden Chain of Romans 8. It is the promise that the good work God began in us will be completed and that Jesus will indeed never allow us to fall from between his fingers. Over and over again, the scriptures speak of God's sovereign call and election on the lives of those he chooses for himself — we are even told that the Holy Spirit will testify to our spirit as to this assurance[223] — it is good news, but it is also news that ought to spur us on to living a life of holiness. Such a life is not only confirmation of the work God has done in us, but it also draws us deeper into relationship with the God we love.

There is a fringe-benefit that also goes along with an understanding of this doctrine. For when we get used to living in this promise, it also should encourage us to step out and take risks for the faith. Indeed, God will never leave or forsake us[224], so what have we to fear?[225] Why fear those who can take our lives but not harm our souls?[226] As Paul writes:

> *For I have been persuaded that neither death nor life, angels nor powers, neither that which has been nor that which will be, neither powers nor heights, neither depths nor any other creature is able to separate us from the love of God in Christ Jesus our Lord. (Romans 8:38-39)*

---

[223] Romans 8:16. Note that were it possible for a genuine believer to fall away, that would make the Holy Spirit guilty of lying.

[224] Hebrews 13:5.

[225] Psalm 23:4; 33:13-19.

[226] Matthew 10:28.

CHAPTER 14
APPLES AND PEACHES AND WORLDVIEW CHANGES

For about two-hundred years, the standard evangelistic model in America has been to offer an "altar-call" at the end of the message, urging people to come forward and dedicate or rededicate their lives to the service of Jesus Christ. While this model has gained popularity and traction in our western culture, it is a model with which Reformed Christians often struggle. The reason for this struggle goes back to our discussion of the sower and the seed — the seed will sprout slightly even in some bad soils, but it will only grow to maturity in soil that has been prepared by the Holy Spirit — that requires a change of life which is unable to be seen or gauged by the act of coming down to the altar and praying the sinner's prayer often spurred on by an emotional appeal. And, sadly, what history has shown is that the majority of the people who come down to such altar calls don't follow-up their profession with a lifestyle that honors Christ Jesus for the rest of their days.[227]

---

[227] Charles Finney (1792-1875) was arguably the American evangelist who popularized the model of the altar call and professions of faith as an evangelistic model. Yet, as he looked back on his life, even he had severe reservations about the overall success of his work. Asa Mahan, a close friend of Finney, wrote to him of these "burned out districts" where Finney had been, describing them in this

So, how do we gauge a conversion? Does scripture offer us a tool to look at our hearts and discern whether our conversion was genuine or the result of a half-hearted conviction that will pass away in time? Can we know that we are elect? While none of us are or will ever be perfect in this life nor are we able to perfectly read the hearts of others, the Bible does give us tools that we can use to help guide us in our introspection and pastoral care.[228]

A Change in Worldview...

Worldview is simply a term that refers to the way we look at and interpret the world around us. The best analogy is that of looking at the world through a set of glasses.[229] The purpose of a pair of glasses is to correct the defective aspects of one's vision so that one can see clearly. If the lenses of the glasses are smudged or damaged, though, one can wind up with all sorts of strange perceptions.

The Greek word that we translate as "repent" is the word μετανοέω (metanoeo)[230] and literally means "to have a change

---

fashion: "The people were left like a dead coal which could not be re-ignited." In a lecture published by Finney in the *New York Evangelist,* Finney wrote of those who had professed faith under his ministry, saying, "The great body of them are a disgrace to religion. Of what use would it be to have a thousand members added to the Church to be just such as are now in it." It is just one more testimony to Jesus' parable of the sower and the seed — genuine revival takes place only in ground that the Holy Spirit has first prepared and while genuine conversion might begin with a profession of faith and a prayer for forgiveness, but it is followed up by a life lived in honor to Christ — as the Heidelberg Catechism would put it — in gratitude for the work of Christ done in our lives.

[228] More, too, will be said on this when we discuss sanctification, but remember, our calling in the Great Commission is to make disciples, not simply converts, though conversion is a first step in discipleship.

[229] For some of us, this is an easy analogy to relate to — for those with the blessing of perfect vision, humor those of us who happened to be your spectacled friends.

[230] This is the verbal form, the noun is μετάνοια (metanoia).

in understanding." You could translate the word as a "change in worldview." In genuine repentance, there is a change in the worldview glasses one wears; the warped lenses are replaced by clear lenses and one rightly turns away from the path of destruction the old worldview had set him upon. This does not mean that every believer sees all things perfectly once repentance takes place — sanctification is a lifelong process — but it does mean that there is a clearly different perspective on the world. And this different perspective on the world ought to lead the believer in a pursuit of different kinds of fruit.[231]

Marks to Identifying This Fruit

Jesus said, you will know a tree by its fruit.[232] The Apostle Paul summarized this fruit as: love, joy, peace, patience, kindness, goodness, faithfulness, gentleness, and self-control.[233] While much can be said about each of these "fruit," my purpose is to simply note two things. First, these are broad categories and are not meant to exhaust the fruit of the believer. Second, Paul uses the collective singular to speak of these fruit — it is not "fruits of the Spirit, but "fruit." In other words, these things on the list are not separate species of fruit like apples and peaches, but instead are aspects of the same fruit that grows in the life of the believer.

Yet, Paul's list here in Galatians is far from the only description of the fruit by which Christians are to be known. For example, in 1 Corinthians 13:4-8a, Paul goes into further depth in describing the nature of the love a Christian should have as part of his fruit. Also, in the beatitudes, Jesus speaks of believers as those who

---

[231] Galatians 5:16-17.
[232] Matthew 7:16-20.
[233] Galatians 5:22-23.

are poor in spirit, mourn over their sins, are meek, hunger and thirst for righteousness, are merciful, pure in heart, and peacemakers, and who face persecution for Jesus' name's sake.[234]

In John's first letter, he goes on at length to demonstrate some of the views that distinguish the life of a believer from the life of an unbeliever. He speaks of one's attitude toward sin[235], one's obedience to the commands of Christ[236], whether he loves his brethren[237], whether he affirms the messiahship and divinity of Christ[238] as well as the humanity of Christ.[239] John goes on to ask professing Christians: "Is righteousness something you seek after and practice?"[240], "Does your conscience condemn you for sin?"[241], "Does your spirit condemn you?"[242], and "Have you overcome the world?"[243] The final statement of John in his first epistle rounds out one more mark of a true believer — we flee from idolatry.[244]

It has been already mentioned, but while people in Christian circles often talk about God's love for us (and it is a worthy subject to speak of and proclaim from the mountaintops indeed!), we often don't talk at length about our love for God. Yet, the Bible regularly

---

[234] Matthew 5:3-12. Note that persecution is an often mentioned sign of a life being lived out in faith — see 1 Peter 4:12-14; 2 Timothy 3:12; Revelation 2:10; 12:17.

[235] 1 John 1:5-10.

[236] 1 John 2:3-6. See also John 14:15,21; 1 John 5:3.

[237] 1 John 2:9-10. Here, John is speaking of believers, not all mankind, though showing love to all mankind can be argued for from other texts.

[238] 1 John 2:22-23.

[239] 1 John 4:2-3.

[240] 1 John 3:4-10.

[241] 1 John 3:19-24.

[242] 1 John 4:1-6. Here, he actually breaks the question up into three categories: view on the incarnation, how you live, and what the world thinks of you.

[243] 1 John 5:5.

[244] 1 John 5:21.

combines the two ideas together.[245] If our love is reflected in our obedience to God's commands, then one can easily use that as a tool for self evaluation. Hear the words of Joshua as he challenges the people:

> *"Only guard closely and do the commandment*
> *and the law that Moses the servant of Yahweh*
> *commanded you: to love Yahweh your God and to*
> *walk in all of his ways, to guard his commandments*
> *and to cleave to him, and to serve him with all of*
> *your heart and with all of your soul."*
> *(Joshua 22:5)*

---

[245] Deuteronomy 5:10.

CHAPTER 15
GOD INITIATES: MAN RESPONDS (THE ORDO SALUTIS)

As theologians have studied the way that Scripture speaks of the conversion of men and women to the Christian faith, they have noticed certain patterns that reflect the way, or order in which, God works in the lives of those he calls to himself. This pattern is referred to in theology as the "Ordo Salutis," which is Latin for, "the order of salvation." Some, theologians like William Perkins and John Bunyan have developed elaborate charts to map out in detail the pathway that a believer is brought to follow as God calls them to faith. Though these elaborate charts are an interesting exploration, our purposes here will be better served with a briefer description of the Reformed view of the Ordo Salutis.

THE DECREE

The Order of Salvation begins before anything that is was brought into being — it begins in eternity prior to creation and lies within the will and decree of God. Within this decree of God there is the decree to elect, for man to fall into sin, and for God to send both

Christ and the Holy Spirit respectively to save and then to sanctify believers, preparing them for heaven.[246]

ELECTION

Though election is properly seen as falling under the decrees of God, theologians typically set this under its own heading. We have discussed election at length already, so I won't explore it further here apart from marking that election, like the Decrees of God, take place prior to God bringing creation into being. The headings that follow, though, reflect the realization of God's election in our lives.

CALLING

This reflects the call of God in the life of a believer. We have discussed the idea that God's call is effectual already, in other words, that when God calls a person to himself, ultimately that person's resistance is broken down and he is brought to Christ by God. That said, this call of God takes a variety of forms, but is typically understood as taking place in four ways. The first form is

---

[246] There are two major views within Reformed circles regarding the theological ordering of these decrees known as "supralapsarnianism" and "infralapsarianism." Note that this ordering is not chronological, but reflects a certain theological priority given to different aspects of God's decree. The Supralapsarian view holds that God chose to elect and that the decision of God to permit the fall was more or less a means to an end. Those holding to the Infralapsarian view would hold that for God to elect without first decreeing the fall (and thus the presence of sin) reflects poorly on the justice of God and thus put forward the position that God decreed to permit the fall and then out of that decreed to elect. Both positions can be found represented within reformed circles through history. What should be noted is that regardless of one's lapsarian view in terms of God's decrees regarding man, one must take a supralapsarian view with respect to God's decree to permit Satan and his angels to fall.

what we call the *Vocatio Realis* or God's call in nature. The psalmist writes that the heavens declare the Glory of God[247] and the Apostle Paul writes that people are without excuse because they see the qualities of the invisible God in his creation.[248] Thus, God places a call before all men that may not be enough to save them, but is enough to hold them responsible. The second form is what we call the *Vocatio Generalis,* which refers to the general call to faith given to all through the preaching of the Gospel. Regularly the evangelist declares to the masses, "Repent and believe!" Some will respond, some will not — it depends on who God is calling to himself.

The third and fourth category shift their focus from external calls to believe to internal calls to faith. The first of these forms is the *Vocatio Creative* or regeneration and the second of the forms is the *Vocatio Verbalis Interna* — our becoming aware of the regeneration and faith that God has worked upon us.

Regeneration

Obviously there is some overlap here with the internal call, but like election, regeneration deserves to stand under its own heading. Regeneration is the new birth of which Jesus speaks when challenging Nicodemus, one of the leaders in the Sanhedron.[249] He tells him that it is impossible to see the kingdom unless one is born again.[250] And why must we be born again? Because, as a result of

---

[247] Psalm 19:1.

[248] Romans 1:18-20.

[249] John 3:3.

[250] Jesus chooses an interesting word in Greek — ἄνωθεν (anothen) — which can mean: "again", "from above", or "from the beginning." While most translators have chosen to use "again" as the meaning based on Nicodemus' response about reentering his mother's womb, it should be noted that all three of these meanings tie neatly into the theology of regeneration for the work of regeneration is done

Adam and Eve's disobedience, we have been born into this world spiritually dead in our sin.[251]

Conversion

Conversion includes two essential parts — sometimes called the "twin sisters" of conversion — you will never find one without the other. The first is genuine saving repentance and the second is saving faith. Both we have spoken of at length already, so we will not explore them further here other than to insist that while there is sometimes a bit of a lag between when faith and repentance become visible in the life of someone coming to faith, where one is genuinely present, the other must not be far away.

Justification

Justification is a legal term that describes how God declares us righteous before the law. This is not because of our works[252], but because we have been made so by the work of Jesus Christ. It should be noted that this is a declarative action — something that takes place at a moment in time — as a judge would do so at the end of a trial; thus, justification is not an ongoing work[253] nor is it

---

upon us by the Spirit — it is a work from above — and, as election is something that takes place before the foundations of the earth, it can be said that regeneration has its origins (in terms of potential) in eternity prior though it is not actualized until the Spirit breathes life into the sin-dead soul.

[251] Ephesians 2:1.

[252] Galatians 2:16; 3:11.

[253] It should be noted that occasionally justification (in the Bible) is used to imply an ongoing work. The definition above is meant to be a very narrow theological definition and does not encompass the totality of the ways the term can be used. Thus, Reformed theologians have historically seen this broader use as encompassing

something that is part of us, but it instead is a completed work which has benefits that have been laid upon us as one might wear a new set of clothing.[254]

Adoption

Along with justification, God makes believers sons and daughters — younger brothers and sisters of his Son, Jesus Christ.[255] This means we are not only given forgiveness, but also an eternal place in his household. A popular misnomer in the broader culture is the belief that because all humans are made in the image of God, all humans are God's children. Yet, the Bible demonstrates the error in that view, instead teaching that it is those who are justified who are children of God and those who reject God who are children of the devil.[256]

Sanctification

Here we find that which is progressive and participatory in the life of the believer. Our sanctification begins immediately after our justification and does not end until we arrive at the grave. We have already discussed sanctification briefly and will discuss

---

aspects of sanctification. An example of this can be found in 1 Corinthians 6:11 where Paul seems to speak of both justification and sanctification in the past tense and the latter ahead of the former. Roman Catholics use this passage to argue that works are necessary to complete the work of Christ; protestants see Paul speaking more generally here than in other places where he is discussing our justification.

[254] Zechariah 3:1-5 portrays just this idea — an idea that theologians refer to as "imputation."

[255] Romans 8:15,23,29; Titus 3:7.

[256] 1 John 3:10

sanctification further in the following chapter, so we will hold off exploring this idea further for now.

GLORIFICATION

When Christians die, our bodies are placed in the ground and our spirits immediately enter into the presence of Christ in glory. When Christ returns to bring his enemies into judgment and to remake this world, then we will be given new bodies and our glorification will be complete — we will become partakers of the divine nature[257] and put on the eternal weight of the glory of Christ.[258]

Models can seem rather wooden and artificial at times, so it is important to note that these models are simply meant to help the believer understand the pathway by which God works in calling the elect to himself. Like the character, Pilgrim, in John Bunyan's classic novel, *Pilgrim's Progress*, the journey that we take from the city of the damned to the celestial city is filled with personal trials and stumbling blocks, but it is a forward path. By simply looking at the map of Pilgrim's travels, one cannot enter into the humanity of these travels, the map simply charts the path. Similarly, the Ordo Salutis is the map that charts our path from election to glorification. The map is important in understanding the theological "big picture" as well as for helping those in your midst who might be behind you in this path walk toward Christ, but the map cannot bring you into contact with the humanity of the events that the map points to, nor can it bring you into communion with the Redeemer. More can be said on all levels of this ordering of salvation, but for our purposes here, the broad map will serve our needs.

---

[257] 2 Peter 1:4.
[258] 2 Corinthians 4:17.

CHAPTER 16
TRIAL BY FIRE – THE WORK OF SANCTIFICATION

I once heard a pastor ask the question as why God refines with fire — fire is painful. He asked, why not refine with water for water is described as the universal solvent. Of course, the answer ought to be clear in the analogy as water takes long periods of time to wear away the hardness of our stone hearts. He then asked, why not with acid? Acid works quickly, let's get it over fast. Yet acid destroys everything to which it is applied. Fire refines. It melts the metals down, exposes the dross, and leaves the metal ready to be recast pure and clean.

Obviously this is an analogy, but it is an analogy that should keep one very important point before us: the process of sanctification is not easy nor is it meant to be. The bottom line is that our heart of stone fights against the new heart that God is developing within us. In many cases, our typical pattern of behavior is not to let go of besetting sin until it is too difficult or painful to hold on to. Thus, God turns up the heat with his spiritual fire.[259]

Unlike Justification, sanctification is a process that will go on for the rest of our lives. In addition, while Sanctification is

---
[259] 1 Peter 1:7.

empowered by the work of the Holy Spirit, it is a process in which we can participate. And for Reformed Christians, this participation with the Holy Spirit is an integral part of our persevering in faith. Furthermore, scripture provides for us tools that equip us in the process.

THE THIRD USE OF THE LAW

John Calvin argued that the Moral Law of God[260] has three primary uses. The first use is that of providing a basis for civil law. All of the laws that God established for his people in the nation of Israel draw their moral basis from the Ten Commandments as they are applied to differing situations in life. Some people struggle with this idea, but imagine for a minute what this world would be like to live in were every man, woman, and child willing to live in accordance with the 10 Commandments — there would be no murder, lying, stealing, adultery, blasphemy, etc... It would be a near-paradise!

The second use of the Law, according to Calvin, is that of demonstrating our sin and driving us to an understanding of our personal need for a savior in Jesus Christ. This is the use that the Apostle Paul speaks of in his letter to the Galatians where he calls the law our pedagogue until the coming of the Gospel.[261] It is a tool in God's hands for evangelism and the humbling of prideful men.

That brings us to what is called "Calvin's Third Use" of the Law. As the Moral Law is a reflection of God's character, the law becomes a tool that the believer can use to examine his or her life to find areas where we can grow to honor God better in our actions. In recent years, the phrase WWJD, standing for "What Would Jesus

---

[260] The Ten Commandments — Exodus 20:1-17; Deuteronomy 5:6-21.
[261] Galatians 3:23-26.

Do?" has grown popular. Calvin would argue that the Law of God, when applied properly, teaches us exactly what Jesus would do in any given situation. Thus, as we week to grow in faith, we apply the law more and more to our own lives to discover areas of growth.

A Petrine Taxonomy

As Peter discusses making our calling and election sure[262], he offers a tiered listing of character traits to build upon that which God has begun in our lives through faith. I refer to this as a taxonomy in that these characteristics are ordered so that one should begin by developing the first then move on to the next and so forth. In Peter's list, he speaks of virtue, knowledge, self-control, steadfastness, godliness, brotherly affection, and agape love.[263] All of these things, Peter says, allows the believer to be fruitful in the work to which God has called them.[264]

The Whole Man

As Original Sin affects the whole man, so too, must sanctification be worked in the life of the whole man. That means sanctification is not just about what we allow our flesh to engage in[265], but it is also about what we allow our minds to dwell upon[266],

---

[262] 2 Peter 1:10. The Greek term here is βέβαιος (bebaios), which pertains to making something abiding or enduring.

[263] 2 Peter 1:5-7. Agape love is a sacrificial love that loves regardless of whether that love is reciprocated on the part of the beloved.

[264] 2 Peter 1:8-9.

[265] Galatians 5:24, noting the emphasis of the flesh along with its passions.

[266] Philippians 4:8.

and in the overall health of our souls.[267] Not an inch of our being is free from the need of this sanctifying work for we are to be holy as our God is holy.[268]

Forgiveness

For many people, it would seem, one of the most difficult aspects of sanctification is their forgiveness of others who have wronged them in one way or another. Yet, Jesus could not be more clear about the connection of our forgiveness of others to our standing before God. This is not merely an aspect of our sanctification, but it is even a sign or a mark that God has begun working faith in us in the first place. Jesus states that if we withhold forgiveness from another, then our Father who is in Heaven will not forgive our sins.[269] In what is known as the Parable of the Unforgiving Servant[270], Jesus goes as far as to say that those who refuse to forgive will be thrown into the torments of hell.[271] Recognize that our forgiveness doesn't so much come out of our character (though our character has something to do with it), but it comes out of the recognition that we have been forgiven far more than we deserve — an eternal debt even — and that if such is the case, how can we begin to hold a debt over the head of another.[272]

---

[267] 1 Peter 2:11.

[268] Leviticus 11:44; 1 Peter 1:14-16.

[269] Matthew 6:14-15.

[270] Matthew 18:23-25.

[271] Matthew 18:34-35. Note that the term that many of our Bibles translate as "jailers" is the word βασανιστής (basanistes), which is an oppressive jailer or tormenter. A better English word to translate this might be "inquisitor." The power of this parable is in recognizing that this debt of the servant is so great that it can never be repaid in an ordinary sense.

[272] It could be argued that a spirit of forgiveness belongs in our discussion of

Sanctification as a Witness to an Unbelieving World

The change of sanctification ought to be visible (sometimes all at once, sometimes gradually over time) to a watching world. Much damage to the Christian testimony has been done by people who are professing Christians but whose life does not reflect the life of Jesus whom they claim to follow. As a result, many people view "church-goers" as hypocritical and self-serving — a critique that is often quite true, though I say so with a great deal of sorrow. This change and transformation in us is not for the end that we attract attention to ourselves or to the church we attend — but to attract attention to Christ Jesus who has done a work in us — changing us in a way that we would have been incapable of changing ourselves. Indeed, it is often through the change that people see in us that they encounter the authentic witness of Jesus Christ[273], thus this participatory process ought to be one into which we enter with reverence and great sincerity[274], resting in the strength of the Spirit of God, not resisting him.

Ultimately, the work of sanctification in our lives is to conform us into the image of Christ[275], which is our ultimate good.[276]

---

the Fruit of the Spirit, and in many ways it does, but recognizing that often this is a long process through which God brings us that serves as a tool of God's sanctification in our lives, I hold that it is best reflected upon here. Learning to genuinely forgive is often the tool by which God most radically changes and remolds us into the image of his Son.

[273] Hebrews 12:14.

[274] Philippians 2:12.

[275] Romans 8:29.

[276] Romans 8:28.

It is a restoration of the *Imago Dei*[277] in our lives that was distorted in the Fall. Yet it is more than just a matter of remaking us like Adam and Eve — we are being remade like Christ and these slight momentary afflictions that cause us to struggle in our sanctification are preparing us for an eternal weight of glory that is beyond anything with which we might be able to compare.[278]

And though this final statement should go without saying, we should be reminded that it is the Scriptures that direct, guide, and instruct us in this process. Nothing that the Spirit does will be contrary to the Word and nothing that we may embrace may be contrary to this Word. We know God, his character, and what he expects from us from the Holy Scriptures — it is our only rule and guide for our faith and for living a life in faith. As John Calvin wrote:

> *"Indeed, the knowledge of God set forth for us in Scripture is destined for the very same goal as the knowledge whose imprint shines in his creatures, in that it invites us first to fear God, then to trust in him. By this we can learn to worship him both with perfect innocence of life and with unfeigned obedience, then depend wholly upon his goodness."*[279]

---

[277] Image of God.

[278] 2 Corinthians 4:17.

[279] Calvin's Institutes I.X.II. Battles Translation.

CHAPTER 17
ONE PEOPLE; TWO COVENANTS

As we bring this survey of Reformed Theology to a close, it is important to speak briefly about what is referred to as Covenant Theology. In fact, it could be legitimately said that all genuine Reformed Theology is Covenant Theology and all Covenant Theology is Reformed Theology, though there are many Godly men who would stand in disagreement on that characterization.

The principle of Covenant Theology is to understand God's design and plan for all humanity throughout history under the overarching theme of covenant — typically understood as a two-covenant system.

WHAT IS A COVENANT?

In principle, a covenant is similar to a contract in that it lays out obligations and responsibilities for two parties, though typically not two equal parties. A king or a landowner, for example, might make up a covenant with those who serve him on this land, exchanging their service and a portion of the crops farmed for protection from raiders or other enemies. Where contracts and covenants separate, though, is in that covenants are made for life and if one broke their end of the covenant, their life would rightly be seen as forfeit.

To reinforce this idea of the binding nature of the covenant, in the ancient near east there were several traditions around the sacrifice of animals and the sealing of the covenant. Genesis 15 records a covenant ceremony that was not a-typical of that which was practiced in Abraham's time, that is apart from one point on which I will elaborate shortly.

Abraham (then still Abram) had begun to fear that he would die without the heir which God had promised.[280] Thus, God chose to take Abraham and to formally ratify this covenantal promise in a very powerful way. God took Abraham out and showed him the stars and promised his offspring would be just as numerous.[281] Then Abraham was commanded to collect animals for a symbolic sacrifice. These animals were collected, cut in half, and laid with halves opposite of each other to create a kind of pathway of blood.[282]

This pathway symbolized the blood of the covenant being made. Scholars differ somewhat as to whether it was both parties or simply the weaker of the parties that would enter into this pathway of blood, but the walking across this path was a statement that said: "If I break this covenant, may what happened to these animals happen to me." Rightly, Abraham should have walked this path, and here is where the wonderful surprise comes. Instead of Abraham walking the pathway, God put him into a deep sleep[283] and God walked through the pathway in Abraham's place in the form of a fire pot and flaming torch. What God was doing in making this covenant, knowing the fallenness of Abraham and of his line, was to promise

---

[280] Genesis 15:2-3.
[281] Genesis 15:6-6.
[282] Genesis 15: 9-10.
[283] Genesis 15:12.

that if Abraham or his people did not live up to the covenant, what happened to these animals would happen to God. That promise, of course, was fulfilled on the cross.

Signs and Mediators

All covenants have signs or symbols of the covenant being made as well as a mediator for the covenant. A mediator's role is to represent those under his authority in the covenant[284] and to intercede for his people when they fall into sin. Ultimately, what we find in scripture are many partial mediators and signs that all ultimately fulfilled in Jesus Christ.

The Covenant of Redemption

As you read Reformed writers, you will sometimes hear them refer to an overarching covenant of Redemption. This is understood to be the inter-Trinitarian covenant between God the Father and God the Son as to the means by which God will send his Son to redeem the fallen elect. This is not a separate covenant, but an umbrella under which the Covenant of Works and the Covenant of Grace exist.

The Covenant of Works

Sometimes this is called a Covenant of Life because it was given in the context of, "do this and live…" Typically, though, in Reformed circles, this is referred to as a Covenant of works

---

[284] We sometimes refer to this as Federal Headship.

because the emphasis here is placed on the obedience of Adam to the covenant being made. This covenant basically laid upon Adam the responsibility that if he and his line were obedient, they could enjoy eternal life in paradise; if they broke the commandment of not eating the fruit of knowledge of good and evil, they would die — spiritually and physically.[285]

THE COVENANT OF GRACE

With the Fall of mankind came the need for a New Covenant to replace the broken one — a covenant that would provide a means to redeem mankind from their fallen state. This covenant is referred to as the Covenant of Grace, for it is by grace we are saved.[286] It is under this covenant that God's people have lived from Adam and Eve's exile from the Garden of Eden until today. And faith in the promised Messiah[287] has been the means by which this covenant is applied to all saints, whether in the Old or the New Testament.[288]

Some object to this assertion on the basis that the Messiah did not come for many generations after the Fall. They say that if Jesus

---

[285] It should be noted that there are two views respecting the duration of this Covenant of Works. Some treat this as a Probationary Covenant never meant as an ongoing covenant under which Adam and his line would live. Under this view, it is believed that had Adam and Eve resisted the temptation of the Devil then they would have been immediately translated into glory — jumping across from Genesis 3 to Revelation 21. The second view is that the Covenant of Works was designed to be a Perpetual Covenant, under which Adam and the generations after him would have lived perpetually in the Garden of Paradise had Adam and Eve not fallen. Obviously, it was God's "Plan A" that Adam and Eve fall, so the matter is a bit speculative in nature, but it is sometimes helpful to understand the nature of the Covenant in these terms.

[286] Ephesians 2:8.

[287] Genesis 3:15 — note that after the fall, Adam and Eve never laid down their head at night to sleep without this promise of a redeemer.

[288] Romans 4:3; Galatians 3:6; James 2:23.

paid the price for sin on the cross of Calvary, then how c[an] Old Testament saints be saved by faith alone in the Messiah? Remember, God is sovereign. Thus what he promises to take place are so sure to take place that we can live and act on those promises even if they have not been fulfilled in our chronological timeline.[289] Thus, it is understood that those who were saved in the Old Testament were saved because they had faith in the promise of the coming Messiah; those who were saved in the Christian era are saved because we have faith in the Messiah who has come — Jesus Christ.

Intermediate Covenantal Language

Within the Old Testament, covenantal language abounds in a variety of contexts. While Dispensational Christians[290] hold that

---

[289] There are spots in scripture where the prophesies uttered of future events are uttered using the past tense form of the verbs in question. This is not always captured in our English translations, but is referred to as the "prophetic perfect" or the "prophetic past" tense. The idea is that the future event is so sure that one might speak of it in the past tense. Examples of this can be found, for example, in Amos 5:2 and John 17:4. In the former case, Amos prophesies the destruction of Israel, in the latter, Jesus speaks of his work being completed even before the coming of the cross.

[290] Dispensationalism is a school of theology that originated with the evangelist, Charles Darby (1800-1882), and popularized by Cyrus Scofield (1843-1921), particularly in his *Scofield Reference Bible.* Scofield took the position that God worked in the lives of his people differently through seven different "dispensations" in history. Thus depending on which dispensation one lived within, one found salvation in different ways. In the 1950s, views in Dispensationalism began to address criticisms raised by Covenantal Theologians, bringing about the rise of what is known as Progressive Dispensationalism, championed by Charles Ryrie (1925-present) and John Walvoord (1910-2002), Dallas Theological Seminary being the modern hub of Progressive Dispensational teaching. Much can be said about the views of those in the Dispensational schools, but in this context, it should be noted that they tend to treat Israel and the Christian Church differently, as if God has two sets of people and different covenantal promises toward each. Covenantal theology treats the church as extending back to Adam and Eve, all saved by faith, and all the bride of Christ and true Israel.

enants, Covenantal Christians hold these each [...] nd cumulative revelations of the Covenant of [...] ltimately pointing to the fullness of the covenant for the Church — true Israel.²⁹¹ As progressive [...] ne Covenant of Grace, they find themselves focusing [...] spects of the covenant and different aspects of Christ's work.

- The Adamic Covenant (Genesis 3:15) — focusing on the promise of that Christ will destroy the Devil and his power. The sign of this covenant was the blood from the animals that God used to clothe Adam and Eve.²⁹²
- The Noatic Covenant (Genesis 8:21-22) — a covenant made with all of creation that God would never again destroy the world by water. The sign of this covenant was the bow of God placed in the clouds.²⁹³
- The Abrahamic Covenant (Genesis 12:2-3; 13:14-17; 15:5,18-21; 17:1-21; 22:16-18; 28:13-15) — a covenant promising a people to be set apart from the rest of the world for blessings and to be a blessing to the nations. The sign of this covenant was circumcision.²⁹⁴
- The Mosaic Covenant (Exodus 20:1-17) — There are multiple promises connected with this covenant, from that of promising to be the God of the people²⁹⁵, to the revealing of his personal name²⁹⁶, to the revealing of his character in

---

[291] See Romans 9:6-8 — not all who are biologically Israel are genuinely Israel (even in Old Testament times), but only those who had faith in the promise of Christ. That is why Paul can say to us that all of the promises of the Old Testament are "yea and amen" in Jesus Christ (2 Corinthians 1:20).

[292] Genesis 3:21.

[293] Genesis 9:12-13.

[294] Genesis 17:11-14.

[295] Exodus 6:7.

[296] Exodus 3:14-15.

the Moral Law[297], to the promise that he would raise up a Messiah that would be a great prophet like Moses.[298] The sign of this covenant was the people's baptism in the Red Sea Crossing.[299]

- The Davidic Covenant (2 Samuel 7:8-16) — The Messiah is promised to be a great king like David. The sign of this covenant is found in Christ's kingship.
- Solomonic Covenant (1 Kings 6:11-13) — This covenant focuses on God's establishing his temple in the midst of his people to dwell with them and to never leave or abandon them. The sign of this is Jesus' coming to dwell[300] with his people as the greater temple[301] and promise never to leave nor forsake his people.[302] Furthermore, Jesus' own resurrection was meant as a sign he was the greater temple.[303]
- The Covenant of Christ — the New Covenant — The fullness of the Covenant of Grace. All of what precedes is designed to point to the new covenant in the blood of Christ whereby men and women who trust in Him will be saved and delivered from this body of death. And the sign of this covenant is the Baptism in the Triune name and Communion at the Lord's Table.

From beginning to end, Scripture presents us as God's people in covenantal relationship with our God. He is our God and

---

[297] The Ten Commandments.
[298] Deuteronomy 18:15.
[299] 1 Corinthians 10:2.
[300] John 1:14.
[301] Matthew 12:6.
[302] Hebrews 13:5.
[303] John 2:19.

we are his people — a people for his own possession.[304] Jesus is the bridegroom and the church of both testaments is the bride[305] — one bride, not two people under multiple covenants, but one people saved under one covenant of grace.

---

[304] 1 Peter 2:9.

[305] John 3:29; Revelation 19:7.

CHAPTER 18
CREDO, ERGO CONFITEOR[306]

Reformed Christians are strongly confessional in their approach to theology. In other words, as a tool for teaching and for clarifying challenging theological questions, confessions of faith have been developed and implemented in church life. These confessions do not replace or supersede the scriptures, they are meant simply to summarize and systematize scriptural ideas. Given our rich confessional history, it seemed odd to me to conclude this book without at least a brief reference to some of the historic confessions that have shaped the Reformed faith through the generations.

The Second Helvetic Confession (1564) — this is a revision of the First Helvetic Confession, as the First Helvetic Confession was believed to be "too Lutheran" in its theology. Thus, Heinrich Bullinger was charged with drafting a replacement (or adaptation). This confession is still considered a primary theological statement for many of the Reformed churches of continental Europe.

---

[306] Latin for, "I believe, therefore I confess."

The Gallic Confession (1559) — This confession was written by Huguenots under the direction of John Calvin and approved by the Reformed Churches in France in secret as the Roman Catholic government of the day was actively engaged in persecuting French protestants.

The Scots Confession (1560) — Written as a confession of faith for the church in Scotland, primarily under the guidance of John Knox.[307]

The Thirty-Nine Articles (1563) — This document was drawn up by the Church in England to establish a theological standard for the Reformational churches of the day. It is considered "loosely Calvinistic," though perhaps not as deeply Calvinistic as many Reformed churches would prefer.

Heidelberg Catechism (1563) — Written by Caspar Olevianus and Zacharius Ursinus, this Catechism was commissioned by Elector Frederick III as a tool to unite the German Reformed and the German Lutheran churches under one theological document. As a result, in areas of theological difference, its wording, it was intentionally designed to leave open room for both Calvinistic and Lutheran views. In the end, the Lutheran churches still held the document to be "too Calvinistic" and it did not gain traction in the Lutheran circles, but has become established as one of the "Three Forms of Unity" in the continental Reformed tradition.[308]

Belgic Confession (1566) — Written by Guido de Bres, a pastor from

---

[307] John Knox (1514-1572) was the leader of the Reformation in Scotland, having studied for a season while in exile in Geneva under John Calvin.

[308] The Three forms of Unity consist of the Heidelberg Catechism, the Belgic Confession, and the Synod of Dort — the combination of the three providing a thoroughly Calvinistic doctrine of faith and practice.

the Netherlands who had studied under Calvin, this confession was designed to be a confessional standard for the churches in the "low countries" of Belgium and the Netherlands, but was also proposed for the underground Reformed church in Spain. It was modeled largely on the Gallic confession and became the confession of faith against which Jacobus Arminius and his students would argue.

Canons of Dort (1619) — As mentioned earlier in this book, when the students of Arminius raised their Remonstrance, the Dutch church leadership met to debate the challenges being raised to the Belgic Confession. Out of this debate came a five-fold document demonstrating the error of the Remonstrance and clarifying Calvinistic soteriology.[309] Delegates not only from the Dutch regions were present in this discussion, but also delegates from across continental Europe and the British Isles.

The Westminster Confession of Faith (1646) — This has become the most widely adopted of the confessions within the non-Continental Reformed movement, today largely seen as Presbyterian in nature. This document contains not only a systematic confession but also a longer and a shorter catechism as teaching tools. Its original purpose was to create a theological document that could unite the Reformed churches in England and Scotland. The Committee was made up of 121 ministers and 30 laymen from various churches and groups in the region. It should be noted that various denominations have edited and revised the original language of this document to serve their specific theological needs and preferences.

The Savoy Declaration (1658) — This was a revision of the Westminster Confession of faith done by the Congregational churches in England which would later cross the seas and is still

---

[309] The doctrine of salvation.

used by certain congregational churches today.

The Helvetic Consensus (1675) — This document was drawn up as a response to the teaching of Moise Amyraut[310] in France. Amyraut taught against the doctrine of Limited Atonement, arguing that Jesus' atonement was theoretically universal, but not practically so because Christ only drew the elect to himself. Though Amyraut's view[311] is accepted in certain branches of the Reformed community, most see it as a compromise of God's justice and sovereignty to argue in this fashion.

The London Baptist Confession of Faith (1689) — This document was a revision of the Westminster Confession done by Reformed Baptist churches in the seventeenth century.

The Calvinist-Methodist Confession of Faith (1823) — As noted earlier, the Methodists who followed George Whitefield were Calvinistic in their theology. When they established a Reformed church, largely centered in Wales, they developed this Confession as their primary theological document, with much of the language borrowed from Westminster.

The Barmen Declaration (1934) — This document was drawn up by Karl Barth[312] in an attempt to unite German Lutheran, Reformed, and United churches against the evils of Adolf Hitler and the Nazi

---

[310] Moise Amyraut (1596-1664) was a French protestant and a professor at the Academy of Saumur. One of Amyraut's most famous students was William Penn, who later went on to found the state of Pennsylvania.

[311] Called Amyraldism.

[312] Karl Barth (1886-1968) was a German Reformed theologian in what is called the "neo-orthodox" school of thought. Neo-Orthodoxy was a response to German liberalism, though it was only a sort of half-way reform, not returning to historic Reformed orthodoxy.

Party. In terms of its structure, it is more practical than theological in nature, though it is an important part of Reformed heritage.

The Belhar Confession (1982) — Like the Barmen Declaration above, this document is focused in terms of addressing practical matters, though in a theological way. Here, not written against Naziism, but against the evils of apartheid and the division of Christ's church along the lines of race and not confession.

Solomon said that of the writing of books there is no end[313] and one might be tempted to ask exactly that question if one were to sit down and read through these and the many other Creeds and Confessions that have adorned the life of the Christian church. Yet, note that Confessions are not something that are new to God's people, even the Bible contains many confessional statements such as Deuteronomy 6:4-9 and 2 Timothy 2:11-13. They are tools by which we can organize our thoughts and confess what we believe to be true. They are also meant as fence-posts to keep out false teachings and to protect those inside of the fence from those who would lead them astray.

---

[313] Ecclesiastes 12:12.

CHAPTER 19
JUST THE BEGINNING

As I bring this book to a close, I want to point out that there is a great deal more that we could be discussing in terms of our Reformed Theology and our Reformed Heritage. Tomes have been written, seeking to plumb the depths of theology, the scriptures, and the application of both to life. This little volume is simply meant as an introduction to the conversation, just barely scratching the surface on some of these ideas but designed to give you the vocabulary and some of the framework particularly to make sense of those theological hills upon which we will take our stand and not compromise. It is meant as a door of introduction — not as the concluding remarks. Reformed thinkers are often criticized for having intense inter-mural debates on the nuances of our theology, that is not intended to divide, but to refine — which even leads us to another Reformed slogan: *semper reformanda,* which means, "always reforming." The slogan is not an invitation to novelty but an honest appeal to be under the perpetual authority of scripture as it refines Christ's church — that is the value that truth holds for us.

It seems appropriate here to close with the words of the Apostle Paul to Timothy:

> *"Be conscientious to present yourself to God as one tested, a workman unashamed, blazing a straight trail in the Word of Truth."*[314]

It is my conviction that such a commitment to Scripture will lead you to the tenets of the Reformed Faith — as it did with me.

---

[314] 2 Timothy 2:15.